THE INDEX OF AMERICA

HOW THE S&P 500 WORKS
& WHY YOU SHOULD INVEST IN IT

Tom Bernard

Library of Congress Control Number: 2026903932
First Printing, San Francisco, CA

Edited By: John Coomer
Designed By: Ed Simkins

www.indexofamerica.com

ISBN (Paperback): 979-8-9947227-1-8
ISBN (Hardback): 979-8-9947227-2-5
ISBN (Digital online): 979-8-9947227-0-1

Take a simple idea and take it seriously.

—Charlie Munger

For my family,
Kaya, Zachary, and Alexa.
With all my love.

WHAT'S MY WHY?

When I was a freshman in college, I was asked to speak to my Grandma Mary and Grandpa Skippy about investing in the stock market. They lived in a small house in Fresno, California, and survived off of a modest pension and social security. They had lived through the Great Depression, and never went to college. Skippy joined the military, then worked at the Okonite factory making the Transatlantic Cable while Mary raised seven kids. They had managed to buy a house and save some money, keeping it invested in a one-year CD (certificate of deposit) at a local bank that they rolled over each year.

I loved them very much and was aware of the math of small but steady growth in income and the ever-rising costs of healthcare and assisted living. It was clear to everyone that they would run out of money. I explained the stock market to them the best way that I could at 19, talking about it going up and down, but mostly up over time. They were both very smart and understood the math of compounding, but they also had lived through the Great Depression and were terrified of the risk of investing and the possibility of losing all their money. They were in their late 70s at the time, and ultimately we agreed that they would keep to their tried and true plan of buying CDs.

This was my first time trying to explain investing and the stock market to someone. I've been trying to figure out how to have that conversation ever since.

As I grew older, I got an internship at PaineWebber building portfolios of mutual funds, then a job as a real estate market analyst focusing on the commercial market. I've had the opportunity to discuss the US equity market and stock investing with co-workers, friends and family over many years. I've even had the chance to teach Personal Finance at the City College of San Francisco, and to give presentations on investing at my office. People typically get the idea of saving and investing, including the different account types like 401k & Roth accounts for retirement. They also usually understand that despite short-term fluctuations, the market generally goes up over time. But when it comes to the actual investments they will buy, that requires more information. I'm here to set the record straight—not all indexes are created equal.

There are many reasons why the S&P 500 is viewed as the highest quality, premier US equity index around the globe. The purpose of this book is to dig deep into the S&P 500 to explain how it works and why you should invest in it.

I'd love to hear your feedback. Please send any thoughts to: indexofamerica@gmail.com.

Thanks for reading.

Tom Bernard

INTRODUCTION

*The market can remain irrational longer
than you can remain solvent.*

—John Maynard Keynes

In 2026, the United States of America celebrates 250 years of existence. America is over 350 million people strong, making up 50 states, one federal district, and five inhabited territories, responsible for producing $30+ trillion per year in economic gross domestic product—about $90,000 per person.[1] This economic power is spread throughout the country, with six of our states having such significant economic might that if they were countries, they would be among the top 20 largest in the world. California would be #4 on its own.[2]

America is made up of many individual economic markets that are bound by a common language, currency, financial system, and set of laws, making it the single largest market in the world. America is the economic engine that you can rely on to grow your wealth in the future.

The ability to compound capital over long periods of

time is the key to your success as an investor. An S&P 500 Index fund (like Vanguard's VFIAX or exchange-traded fund (ETF) equivalent, VOO) allows you to invest at a low annual cost—which means more of your money can stay invested and compound. Once you've identified an investment that consistently turns $ invested into more $$, you want to do that as soon as you can, for as long as you can, at the lowest cost possible.

Over 10, 15, and 20-year periods ending 12.31.2024, the S&P 500 has beaten 97%+ of actively managed large-capitalization core funds on an after-tax basis.[3] Significantly, in his 2013 annual letter to shareholders, Warren Buffett laid out his instructions for how he wants his wife to invest her money when he dies[4]:

"Put 10% of the cash in short-term government bonds and 90% in a very low-cost S&P 500 Index fund. (I suggest Vanguard's.) I believe the trust's long-term results from this policy will be superior to those attained by most investors—whether pension funds, institutions or individuals—who employ high-fee managers."

My goal with this book is to shed some light on the S&P 500; how it works and why you should invest in it. I hope there is something in the following pages that can improve your understanding of the S&P 500, as well as provide some guidance and comfort during times of uncertainty that will help you to hold on to your investments through trying times—and just do nothing when all you want to do is sell. Remember that money is made not in the buying or selling, but in the waiting (via compounding)…and waiting can be very hard to do.

This book will cover how the S&P 500 came to be, the

required criteria for a company to be eligible for inclusion in the index and some of the factors considered when determining exactly which company makes it in, the calculation methodology, the evolution of the selection criteria and the calculation over time, as well as the role that the S&P 500 plays in financial markets. I'll discuss the index's attributes and historic performance along with the role that the S&P 500 plays in the $65 billion+ investment portfolio of one of the nation's top-performing public pensions—the Nevada Public Employees' Retirement System. I'll wrap up with a brief discussion of the corporate life cycle, the role of share repurchases in returning capital to owners, and how these concepts can help explain the persistent increase in earnings per share of S&P 500 constituents over time.

The thing to remember as you read this is that there are different systems at work (S&P Global, SPDJI, CME Group, GICS, MSCI, the S&P 500 Index Committee, and constituent companies), with each being optimized to generate the best overall outcome and sustainable operating performance.

Each set of stakeholders is doing their best to drive exceptional results. When you purchase a fund that tracks the S&P 500, like VFIAX from Vanguard, all of the knowledge and experience of these world-class organizations, and everyone that works there, is working for you. To top it off, the mechanics of buying, selling, reporting, etc. are done by one of the largest and most efficient financial organizations in the world, at a very low cost.

S&P 500 2025—5 Fun Facts

1. The 2025 total investment return for the S&P 500 was 17.88%. Total returns for the past 3, 5, 10, 15, and 20 years are as follows:

S&P TOTAL ANNUAL AVERAGE INVESTMENT RETURNS	
12 Months	17.88%
3 Years	23.01%
5 Years	14.42%
10 Years	14.82%
15 Years	14.06%
20 Years	11%

Table I-1

2. The S&P 500 price change in 2025 contributed 16.39% to the total investment return. Reinvested dividends contributed the other 1.49%.

3. The so-called "Mag 7" (Magnificent Seven) stocks (Apple, Microsoft, Amazon, Alphabet (Google), Nvidia, Meta (Facebook) and Tesla) contributed 7.52% to the total investment return in 2025. The other 493 stocks contributed 10.36%.

4. The Information Technology sector made up over 45% of the 2025 total investment return, followed by Communications Services at just under 18% and Financials at almost 12%.

5. S&P 500 corporate earnings are returned to shareholders as buybacks or dividends. For the 12 months ended September 2025, reported earnings were estimated to be $1,994 billion. Dividends paid out were $665 billion and buybacks $1,020 billion. That means a total of $1,685 billion (or 85% of the earnings) was returned to shareholders. The remaining $309 billion (15%) was retained by the companies.[5]

Interested Parties

<u>S&P Global Inc.</u>
A provider of credit ratings, benchmarks, analytics, and workflow solutions.

<u>CME Group Inc.</u>
Provides services that enable clients to trade futures, options, cash and over-the-counter (OTC) products, optimize portfolios, and analyze data.

<u>S&P Dow Jones Indices (SPDJI)</u>
A joint venture owned by S&P Global (73%) and CME Group (27%). SPDJI is a global index provider maintaining a wide variety of valuation and index benchmarks.

<u>MSCI Inc. (formerly Morgan Stanley Capital International)</u>
Products and services include indexes; portfolio construction and risk management tools, environmental, social, and governance (ESG) and climate solutions; and private asset data and analysis.

<u>Global Industry Classification Standard (GICS)</u>
Formed in 1999 by SPDJI and MSCI, GICS created a set of definitions that enable comparisons across countries, regions and globally. GICS allows multiple levels of analysis, ranging from the most general Sectors to the most specialized Sub-Industries. GIC assigns each company to a sub-industry based on the company's principal business activity.

<u>SPDJI Index Committee</u>
Constantly evaluating the index to make sure that its eligibility

criteria and calculation methodology make it the premier benchmark and leading indicator of the U.S. economy.

<u>Constituent Companies</u>
Striving every day to be the best in class so that they can earn or keep their spot in the index.[6]

Definitions

S&P Global Broad Market Index

Rules based, global index that has been fully float adjusted since 1989, covers 14,000+ stocks including both developed and emerging markets.

S&P Total Market Index

A float-adjusted market capitalization weighted index that includes almost 4,000 U.S common equities.

S&P 500

A float-adjusted market capitalization weighted index composed of 500 constituent companies that measures the performance of the large cap-segment of the U.S. market defined as having a market capitalization of at least $22.7 billion. Captures the market capitalization from the largest down to the 85th percentile of the S&P Total Market Index.

S&P Completion Index

Made up of all members of the S&P Total Market Index, except those in the S&P 500.

S&P MidCap 400

A float-adjusted market capitalization weighted index composed of 400 constituent companies that measures the performance of the mid-cap segment of the U.S. market defined as having a market capitalization of at least $8.0 billion and less than $22.7 billion. Captures market capitalization of the 85th to 93rd percentile of the S&P Total Market Index.

S&P SmallCap 600

A float-adjusted market capitalization weighted index composed of 600 constituent companies that measures the performance of the small-cap segment of the U.S. market defined as having a market capitalization of at least $1.2 billion and less than $8.0 billion. Captures the market capitalization of the 93rd to the 99th percentile of the S&P Total Market Index.

S&P Composite 1500

A float-adjusted market capitalization weighted index composed of all constituent companies that measures the performance of all three market size segments: the S&P 500, S&P MidCap 400, and S&P SmallCap 600.[7]

Frequency of Decisions/Processes

Annually

- The S&P Total Market Index is reconstituted annually—all eligible securities are selected to form the index.
- At least once every 12 months, the Index Committee reviews its methodology to confirm that stated objectives are achieved and the data and methodology are effective. If necessary, the Index Committee may solicit feedback from outside parties.
- GICS classifications are also reviewed annually.

Quarterly

- The share counts and float adjusted market capitalization weights are updated for each constituent company.
- Market capitalization ranges for the S&P 1500 Composite Index are reviewed. If the indicated range differs from the current range by 10% or more, then the Index committee will consider adjusting them. Updates are effective immediately when announced.
- Rebalancing of the indexes: Securities that have undergone a change in the past quarter are eligible to be added to the index subject to a reference date that is five weeks prior to the rebalancing effective date.

Monthly

- The Index Committee maintains the indices and meets monthly to review pending corporate actions that may impact the index constituents, review the index composition to the overall market, review significant market events, discuss companies being considered for addition or removal, and update index policy as needed.

<u>Ad-Hoc</u>

- Companies may be added or removed from the index at any time.
- GICS classification changes occur when there is a corporate action that changes a company's primary business activity. Companies may also request a review.
- SPDJI and MSCI review the GICS structure periodically.

S&P Development Timeline

<u>1860</u>

Henry Varnum Poor starts Poor's Publishing.

<u>1906</u>

Luther Lee Blake starts the Standard Statistics Bureau.

<u>1923</u>

Standard Statistics Co. creates a 233-company market capitalization-weighted composite index, updated weekly.

<u>1926</u>

Standard Statistics Co. develops a market capitalization-weighted index of 90 stocks, updated daily.

<u>1941</u>

Poor's Publishing merges with Standard Statistics Co. to form Standard & Poor's (S&P).

Post-merger, the weekly composite index was increased to 402 stocks with 350 industrials in the 1940s.

<u>Early 1950s</u>

The weekly composite index expands to 480 stocks—420 industrials, 40 utilities, 20 railroads.

<u>March 4, 1957</u>

S&P 500 Index launched:

- 500 companies—425 industrials, 50 utilities, 25 railroads.
- Market cap-weighted.

- Trading begins at 44.22.
- First computer-generated index.
- Melpar, Inc. designs S&P's initial electronic calculation system and process.

1962

Ultronic Systems becomes the compiler and early technological partner for index calculation.

S&P launches Compustat.

1973

One of the first institutional indexed funds launches based on the S&P 500: the Wells Fargo Stagecoach Fund.

August 31, 1976

The first S&P 500 retail index mutual fund (Vanguard) launches to democratize access to market returns for individual investors and fuel passive investing.

April 21, 1982

S&P 500 futures begin trading on the Chicago Mercantile Exchange (CME) to provide an institutional tool for hedging and speculation, increased index liquidity, and prominence.

July 1, 1983

S&P 500 options begin trading on the Chicago Board Options Exchange (CBOE), adding further risk management and trading capabilities, as well as deepening market integration.

<u>1986</u>

S&P 500 Index update increased to every 15 seconds (the current frequency is 1 second) to enhance real-time market tracking and responsiveness.

S&P partners with Reuters.

<u>January 22, 1993</u>

First ETF to track the S&P 500—the SPDR S&P 500 ETF Trust (SPY) launched—revolutionizing index investing with stock-like trading flexibility, massively growing the assets tracking the S&P 500.

<u>September 9, 1997</u>

S&P 500 E-mini futures contract introduced on the CME, broadening access to S&P 500 futures and boosting liquidity.

<u>1999</u>

Global Industry Classification Standard (GICS) developed with Morgan Stanley Capital International (MSCI) to create standardized industry classifications and enhance analytical consistency. This is currently managed by SPDJI and MSCI.

<u>2003</u>

The world's first S&P 500 equal weight ETF launched.

<u>2004</u>

First volatility derivatives launched (VIX futures) on the CBOE.

2005

Transition to float-adjusted market capitalization weighting, a major methodological shift to more accurately reflect the investable market and enhance benchmark integrity.

2012

The SPDJI formed as a joint venture, owned 73% by S&P Global and 27% by the Chicago Mercantile Exchange (CME) Group.

Ongoing

The evolution of index eligibility criteria (market capitalization, profitability, etc.) ensures that it remains representative of the large-cap U.S. companies.[8]

CHAPTER 1

STANDARD & POOR'S GLOBAL HISTORY: ORIGIN–1957

The story begins in the 19th century with Henry Varnum Poor, who founded Poor's Publishing in 1860. His firm initially gained prominence by publishing comprehensive investor guides, with a particular focus on the rapidly expanding railroad industry. This early venture into systematized financial information established a demand for reliable data and analysis, a precursor to the sophisticated market indicators that would follow. The focus on specific sectors, like railroads, represented an initial attempt to categorize and understand distinct segments of the investment landscape, a foundational concept for later, broader market indices.

Separately, the Standard Statistics Bureau was founded in 1906, later becoming the Standard Statistics Company. This organization took more direct steps toward modern indexation. In 1923, it developed its first stock market index, a relatively broad measure consisting of 233 U.S. company stocks, with its value computed on a weekly basis. This was a significant innovation, moving beyond the analysis of individual securities to offer a composite view of a substantial portion of the U.S. stock market. The weekly calculation, however, reflected the technological and data processing limitations of the era.

Recognizing the growing need for more timely market information, Standard Statistics introduced a more focused 90-stock index in 1926 that was computed daily. This index, referred to as the "Composite Index", was specifically designed as a more manageable subset of stocks to facilitate the more frequent dissemination of market indicator information. The shift to daily computation was a critical advancement, catering to a financial community that increasingly required up-to-date market intelligence. The reduction in the number of constituents from 233 to 90 was likely a pragmatic compromise, balancing the desire for representative breadth with the then-existing capabilities for daily data collection and calculation. This 90-stock index is a direct ancestor of the S&P 500, with its historical daily data back to 1928 (and monthly to 1926) later linked to the S&P 500 to provide a continuous historical record.

The progression from industry-specific guides to broader, more frequently calculated stock indices demonstrates a clear evolutionary trend. This was driven by the increasing complexity of financial markets and a corresponding investor demand for more sophisticated tools for market assessment. The limitations inherent in earlier, narrower, or less frequently updated indicators naturally spurred the development of more advanced measures like the 90-stock daily index. This iterative development process, moving from a weekly 233-stock index to a daily 90-stock index, highlights an early understanding within Standard Statistics Co. that a truly useful market indicator must carefully balance the breadth of its coverage with the practical necessities of timely calculation and dissemination—a principle that remains relevant in the index's design today.

The Merger

A pivotal moment in this lineage occurred in 1941 when Poor's Publishing merged with Standard Statistics Company to form Standard & Poor's (S&P). This strategic union brought together the strengths of two established financial information firms, creating a more formidable entity. Poor's Publishing contributed its long-standing reputation and experience in providing investor guidance, while Standard Statistics brought its pioneering expertise in index construction and bond ratings.

The newly formed Standard & Poor's Corporation positioned itself as a comprehensive provider of financial information and analysis. This consolidation of expertise and resources under a single, respected brand was crucial. It created an organization with the scale, credibility, and technical capacity necessary to develop and maintain increasingly sophisticated financial products, including the market indices that would define its legacy. The S&P name itself became synonymous with trusted financial data, a vital attribute for any entity aspiring to produce a benchmark that would gain widespread market acceptance. This merger underscores how corporate evolution and strategic alliances can serve as critical enablers of innovation. Without this consolidation, the resources and combined expertise required for an undertaking as ambitious as the S&P 500 might have been fragmented or delayed, potentially altering the course of benchmark development in the U.S. financial markets.

The groundwork laid by its predecessor entities and the strategic 1941 merger set the stage for Standard & Poor's to introduce a transformative market benchmark. The year 1957 marked the official birth of the S&P 500 as it is widely recognized today, an index designed to offer a more comprehensive and economically meaningful measure of the U.S. stock market.

On Monday, March 4, 1957, Standard & Poor's expanded its existing index framework to encompass 500 companies, renaming it the S&P 500 Stock Composite Index.[9] This expansion was a deliberate and significant undertaking, driven by a recognized need within the financial community for a more comprehensive and representative benchmark than existing alternatives, most notably the Dow Jones Industrial Average (DJIA), which tracked only 30 stocks.[10] The S&P 500 was explicitly designed to be a broad-based index reflecting the performance of leading U.S. equities across a diverse range of industries.

The selection of 500 companies was carefully considered to ensure extensive market coverage. The initial composition comprised 425 industrial, 25 railroad, and 50 utility stocks. This carefully curated list of companies collectively accounted for over 90% of the total market value of U.S. equities listed on the New York Stock Exchange at that time.[11] The explicit aim was to provide a far more accurate and holistic reflection of the U.S. stock market's performance and composition. This ambition to capture such a dominant share of market value underscored the index's design philosophy: to be a truly encompassing barometer of American corporate performance.

A crucial methodological decision that distinguished the S&P 500 from its inception was its use of market-capitalization weighting. This meant that each company's influence on the index's value was directly proportional to its total market value, calculated by multiplying its stock price by the number of its outstanding shares. This approach contrasted sharply with the price-weighting mechanism of the Dow Jones Industrial Average (DJIA), where higher-priced stocks had a greater impact regardless of the company's overall size or economic significance. Market-capitalization weighting is widely considered a more economically intuitive and representative method for constructing a market index, as it better reflects the actual economic footprint and investor interest in the constituent companies.

The launch of such a complex index, involving 500 stocks and market-capitalization calculations, was made feasible by technological advancements. The S&P 500's introduction in 1957 was enabled by an electronic calculation method developed by Melpar, Inc., a Boston-based firm. This made the S&P 500 the first major computer-generated stock market index, reportedly utilizing electronic punch cards for its computations. This "electronic wizardry" (as S&P termed it) allowed for far more efficient and timely calculations than previously possible. With this new technology, S&P could perform index calculations much more rapidly, enabling the dissemination of index values on an hourly basis throughout the trading day. This frequency of updates was a significant improvement, providing investors with a more dynamic measure of market movements.

To ensure historical continuity and analytical utility, Standard & Poor's also compiled an 80-page document providing historical data for the new index. This included daily figures for the S&P 500 and its subgroup indices (industrial, railroad, utility) dating back to 1928, with weekly data available for 1926–1927, effectively linking the new 500-stock index to the earlier 90-stock Composite Index. This provision of a substantial historical record was essential for establishing the credibility of the S&P 500 and allowing for meaningful long-term market analysis from its outset.

The advent of early computing technology was critical

to the S&P 500's creation. While the conceptual need for a broader, more representative market index was apparent, the practical challenges of managing data for 500 companies, calculating market-capitalization weights, and updating values frequently were immense with pre-electronic methods. Melpar Inc.'s electronic calculation system provided the technological breakthrough necessary to overcome these hurdles. This synergy between financial insight and technological capability was foundational, marking the S&P 500's birth as an early example of financial technology in action.

The initial composition of the S&P 500 in 1957 reflected the prevailing structure of the mid-20th century American economy. It was dominated by large industrial corporations, such as General Electric, U.S. Steel, and DuPont, which were giants of that era. The breakdown of 425 industrials, 25 railroads and 50 utilities mirrored the key sectors driving economic activity at the time. Notably, financial stocks had a limited presence in the initial index, primarily consisting of consumer finance companies rather than the large commercial banks or investment firms that would become more prominent later. This composition provided a snapshot of an economy heavily reliant on manufacturing, heavy industry, and regulated utilities.

The S&P 500's design offered a stark contrast to the Dow Jones Industrial Average, the most widely recognized U.S. stock market indicator at the time. The DJIA comprised only 30 stocks and employed a price-weighting methodology, as it still does today. The S&P 500, with its 500 constituents and market-capitalization weighting, was engineered to provide a more comprehensive and, many argued, more accurate measure of overall market performance. The DJIA's price-weighting could lead to distortions, where a high-priced stock of a smaller company could have more influence on the index value than a lower-priced stock of a much larger, more economically significant company. The S&P 500's market-cap weighting avoided this, ensuring that companies with greater total market values had a proportionally larger impact on the index. Furthermore, the sheer breadth of the S&P 500, covering a significant majority of the U.S. market capitalization, offered a more diversified and therefore more stable representation of market trends compared to the concentrated nature of the DJIA.

This deliberate design for superior market representation was a key element of the S&P 500's value proposition from its launch. By encompassing a broad array of leading companies across various industries and weighting them by their economic scale, the S&P 500 aimed to overcome the perceived limitations of narrower or methodologically different benchmarks. This established a new standard for index construction, emphasizing comprehensive coverage and economic relevance, a philosophy that has profoundly influenced how market performance is measured and understood not only in the U.S., but globally.

CHAPTER 2

FINANCIAL TECHNOLOGY & THE CREATION OF THE S&P 500

The American economy of the 1950s was an engine of unprecedented expansion. In the wake of World War II, the nation experienced a period of remarkable prosperity, characterized by burgeoning industrial might and the rise of a robust middle class with newfound disposable income. This economic dynamism fueled a surge in public participation in the stock market, creating a pressing demand for more sophisticated, reliable, and comprehensive tools for financial analysis. For a growing cohort of investors and the professionals who advised them, the existing market yardsticks at the time (the DJIA, SP90, and Amex) were proving inadequate. The market was in need of a better measure.

The most prominent of these was the Dow Jones Industrial Average (DJIA). While a household name, the DJIA was increasingly viewed by financial professionals as a narrow and potentially misleading representation of the U.S. economy's true breadth and vigor. Its reliance on a small sample of just 30 companies and its price-weighted methodology—which gave undue influence to stocks with high share prices regardless of the company's overall size—were significant flaws in an era of rapid diversification and growth.

The creation of the Standard "500" on March 4, 1957, was not a simple expansion of an existing list but a revolutionary act of financial engineering. It was the culmination of the philosophical vision of Lew Schellbach, the meticulous data architecture of George Olsen, and a critical technological leap devised by Dr. John Hansen of Melpar, Inc., which together created and enabled the foundational benchmark for modern investment management. This narrative provides a brief explanation of this pivotal work within the context of this transformative moment in financial history.

Lew Schellbach

Lewis "Lew" Schellbach was the principal architect and driving force behind the S&P 500, a role that earned him the "Father of the S&P 500" moniker. His position at Standard & Poor's was a unique amalgamation of economist, editor, and Public Relations Director, affording him a panoramic view of the financial landscape. This synthesis of roles was critical: he possessed the analytical acumen to diagnose the shortcomings of existing indices, the editorial authority to champion a new solution internally, and the public-facing platform to evangelize its benefits to the financial world.

The dominant index of the era, the DJIA, with its small basket of 30 stocks, was more susceptible to the volatile swings of a few high-priced components, making it a less stable barometer. A broader, more comprehensive index of 500 leading companies, weighted by their actual economic footprint (market capitalization), was inherently more stable and a truer reflection of the productive economy. The S&P 500 can be understood as a tool that measures the health of the industrial and commercial economy.

On February 27, 1957, it was Schellbach who stood before 35 of the nation's top financial writers at the Lawyers Club in New York City to unveil the new Standard "500". His ability to articulate the index's purpose and superiority was paramount to its launch. His stature endured for decades; as an executive vice president in the 1970s, he was still a go-to source for major publications like Time magazine for commentary on market psychology, a testament to his lasting influence as a leading voice for Standard & Poor's and the market itself.

The vision for a broad, frequently calculated market index could not have been realized without a crucial technological breakthrough. The emergence of the S&P 500 in 1957 was explicitly 'made possible' and "enabled" by a new electronic calculation method developed by Melpar, Inc. This technology was the linchpin that allowed Standard & Poor's to leapfrog the computational barriers that had previously relegated its broad composite index to slow, manual, weekly updates.

John Hansen

Dr. John Hansen was part of the Boston-based Applied Research

Laboratory of Melpar, Inc., an aerospace engineering company. This group was responsible for complex engineering projects that required the extraction of meaningful signals from massive datasets—a skill set directly transferable from radar tracking to stock market indexing.

According to a New York Times article, Dr. Hansen became "fascinated with the possibilities of the Datatron electronic computer, made by the Burroughs Corporation" in 1955.[12] He and his team conducted some experiments and in 1956 "went to Standard & Poor's with their findings". Standard & Poor's obtained the cooperation of the New York Stock Exchange (NYSE) and the Western Union Telegraph Company. They obtained permission to use the NYSE's ticker and the loan of a tape-punching device called a reperforator from Western

Analyst works with the Datatron, which performs the calculation to generate the new hourly index.

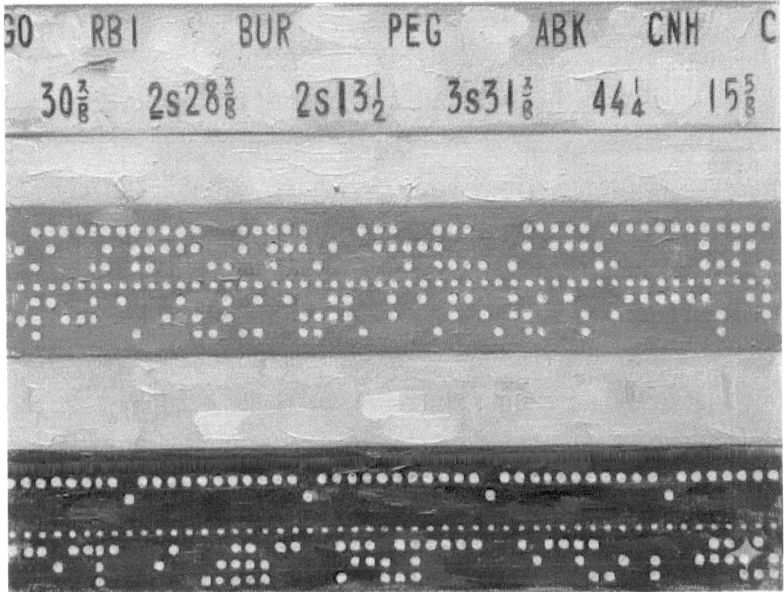

Three tapes were required:
Top — NYSE ticker Tape of market data.
Middle — Output from Reperforator
Bottom — 4-Channel tape fed into the Datatron after data cleansing and conversion

Union. The impulses that activated the NYSE's ticker were fed into the reperforator, which reproduced the kind of perforated tape punched out by the Exchange ticker room in the Boston Laboratory. This was the beginning of a new process in financial technological innovation that combined an existing process of taking a data feed from the stock exchange, transmitting it over the telegraph line, and then converting the stock price data onto a paper tape.

The reperforator generated a six-channel tape, while the Datatron used a four-channel tape. So a converter had to be devised to get the tape into the Datatron. This complex instrument cut out bid-and-ask quotations and cash sales, recording only regular deals in the 500 common stocks of the new index. This was significant because there were over 1,100 stocks on the exchange at the time, so they had created something new—a piece of software to remove the unnecessary information or noise in order to get a purer signal of the relevant stock data.

Additionally, the new system remembered the most recent trade in each stock. At any moment, a button could be pressed and a composite average learned. The Datatron multiplied each price by the outstanding shares, and then computed the index. The answer was then sent by Teletype. The new indexes for industrials, rails, and utilities could be made available to investors only a minute or so after any hour.

The Standard 500 would not have been possible without the technical innovation of Dr. John Hansen and his team, who combined the disparate systems, designed the process, and programmed the machines.

George Olsen

While Lew Schellbach was the public visionary, and Dr. John Hansen and the Melpar team were the technical wizards, George Olsen was the indispensable partner who built the index's operational and analytical backbone. Identified as Schellbach's colleague, Olsen co-led the critical and painstaking process of selecting the inaugural 500 companies. Their method was not a simple quantitative screen but a discretionary review; they meticulously 'combed the list' of stocks on the New York Stock Exchange to identify the most 'meaningful' and representative firms, deliberately filtering out those that were too thinly traded or garnered insufficient public interest.

Olsen's most profound and strategically vital contribution, however, was the creation of the index's historical record. He led a 'crew' at Standard & Poor's in the monumental task of assembling an 80-page document that provided a complete history of the new index before it even launched. This document contained daily closing values for the S&P 500 and its subgroups back to 1928, with weekly data extending back to 1926.

This project was a masterstroke of strategic planning that endowed the S&P 500 with immediate authority and utility. A new financial instrument launched without historical context is mere curiosity. Professional security analysts—the primary target audience for the new index—rely on extensive historical data for trend analysis, valuation models, and risk assessment. By undertaking the laborious, pre-digital database task of back-testing and compiling nearly three decades of data, Olsen's team armed the S&P 500 with a rich, usable history from its very first day. The subsequent distribution of this 80-page book to security analysts, members of the American Stock Exchange, and other key market participants was a deliberate and highly effective marketing strategy. It provided the professional community with the exact tools needed to immediately integrate the S&P 500 into their workflows, benchmark their portfolios against it, and ultimately adopt it as the new standard. Olsen's role transcended that of a mere statistician; he was the architect of the index's credibility and the catalyst for its rapid acceptance across Wall Street.

The S&P 500

The creation of the S&P 500 was a direct response to the clear deficiencies of existing market measures. The DJIA was price-weighted and used a methodology that distorted the influence of its components. A company with a high stock price commanded a greater weight in the index regardless of its overall size or economic importance, while a larger company with a lower stock price had less influence. Furthermore, with only 30 stocks, it failed to capture the growing diversity of the American economy.

Standard & Poor's itself had predecessor indices, each with its own limitations. The S&P 90-Stock Composite Index, launched in 1926 and calculated daily, was an important step forward. It comprised 50 industrial, 20 railroad, and 20 utility stocks. However, it was viewed primarily as a large-cap index and was not broad enough to be a truly comprehensive market proxy. Concurrently, S&P maintained a much broader S&P Composite Index, which by 1957 included 480 stocks (420 industrials, 20 railroads, and 40 utilities) The critical flaw of this broader index was its calculation frequency: it was computed only once a week, on Wednesdays, making it unsuitable for the increasingly dynamic needs of daily market tracking.

The S&P 500 was conceived as the solution to this fundamental dilemma of breadth versus frequency. The market required the comprehensiveness of the 480-stock weekly index but with the high-frequency calculation of the 90-stock daily index. The new "500" was engineered to synthesize these two previously mutually exclusive attributes. The practical constraints of the endeavor are highlighted by the fact that the historical data for the S&P 500, compiled by Olsen's team, was built upon the daily history of the S&P 90 back to 1928. This was a choice born of necessity—it was the only available data source—not an admission of the S&P 90's superiority.

With Melpar's system, the complex calculations required

for a 500-stock, market-cap-weighted index could be performed with unprecedented speed, allowing for updates on an hourly, intraday basis. This new efficiency was so powerful that S&P could have, in theory, tracked every single stock listed on the New York Stock Exchange (1,100). This fact reveals a critical decision point in the index's creation. Schellbach and Olsen were not simply letting technology dictate the final product. Instead, they harnessed this new computational power to enable their curated, human-driven vision. The Melpar system provided the raw processing capability, but it was the expert judgment of Schellbach and Olsen that provided the wisdom, shaping the index into a tool that was comprehensive but also liquid, meaningful, and truly representative of the market's leaders.

The selection of the 500 companies was a testament to the blend of art and science that defined the project. It was a discretionary, committee-based process, a tradition that continues at S&P to this day and stands in contrast to the purely formulaic inclusion rules used by other index families. Schellbach and Olsen deliberately sought to build a portfolio of industry leaders, ensuring the index was not only representative of the market as a whole, but was also composed of liquid, actively traded securities.

The result of their careful curation was an index that, despite its finite number of constituents, achieved immense breadth. As highlighted in Chapter 1, the initial 500 stocks accounted for over 90% of the total market capitalization of all U.S. stocks, giving the index the statistical authority to act as a proxy for the entire American stock market. This inaugural composition of the index provides a clear snapshot of the post-war American economy. This sectoral breakdown would remain fixed until 1976, when financial companies were first added, marking the index's first major evolution to reflect changes in the U.S. economy.

Perhaps the most profound and enduring innovation of the S&P 500 was its use of a market capitalization-weighted methodology. Under this system, each company's influence on the index's value is directly proportional to its total market value—calculated as its stock price multiplied by the number of shares outstanding. This stood in stark contrast to the DJIA's price weighting.

The difference is fundamental. In a price-weighted index like the Dow, a company with a $100 stock price and 1 million shares outstanding (market capitalization: $100 million) would have five times the influence of a company with a $20 stock price and 10 million shares outstanding (market capitalization: $200 million). This is despite the fact that the second company is twice as large and has a greater economic footprint. In the market-cap-weighted S&P 500, the second, larger company would rightly have twice the influence of the first. This methodological choice ensured the S&P 500 was a more accurate, representative, and fundamentally sound mirror of the U.S. economy than any major index that came before it. It measured economic significance, not arbitrary stock price levels. This superior design is the primary reason the S&P 500 ultimately supplanted the DJIA as the preferred benchmark for institutional investors and financial professionals.

The S&P 500's design—broad, representative, and based on a clear methodology—made it the perfect vehicle for the nascent theories of passive investing that were gaining traction in academia. The index provided a tangible, investable proxy for "the market". Eventually, an investment vehicle was created to provide access to the index for investors:

- In 1976, John Bogle's Vanguard launched the first index mutual fund available to retail investors, the Vanguard 500 Index Fund, designed to specifically track the S&P 500.

- In 1993, the first major U.S. exchange-traded Fund (ETF), the SPDR S&P 500 ETF (ticker: SPY), began trading, further democratizing access to the index and revolutionizing portfolio management.

The work of Lew Schellbach and George Olsen in 1957 was far more than the creation of a new list of stocks; it was the establishment of a new paradigm for measuring economic reality. Schellbach's philosophical vision for a stable, representative market measure, combined with Olsen's meticulous data architecture and enabled by the computational power of Melpar's technology, produced the most important financial benchmark of the 20th century. They constructed the intellectual and data-driven infrastructure upon which modern portfolio theory, the passive investing revolution, and trillions of dollars in global assets now rest. The Standard "500" was the answer to a market in need of a measure, and its enduring, evolving legacy continues to shape the financial world in profound ways.

CHAPTER 3

THE S&P 500 TODAY

The total value of the S&P 500 constituent companies at the end of 2025 was approximately $61 trillion. The fair market value of publicly traded U.S. equities was approximately $66 trillion, and the value of accessible publicly traded global equities was approximately $107 trillion.[13]

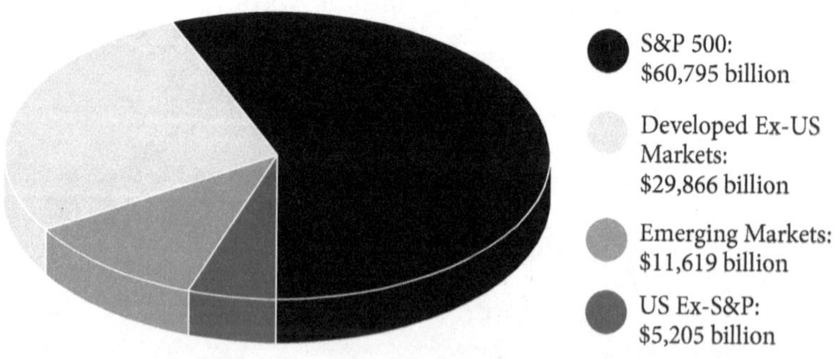

The $107–Trillion S&P Broad Market Index at 12/31/2025 [14]

Diagram 3-1

Using these figures, the S&P 500 represents 92% of the fair market value of U.S. stocks and about 57% of global stocks.

The S&P 500 is the basis of a large trading "ecosystem". This ecosystem generated over $278 trillion in trading volume in 2024.[15] One of the primary benefits is price discovery. There are now products tracking the S&P 500, including futures, options, exchange-traded funds, and exchange- traded products that trade around the world almost 24 hours a day. These products have their own markets and stakeholders that are able to express a view of the market through these products. They also allow risk to be transferred from one party to another, making markets more efficient.

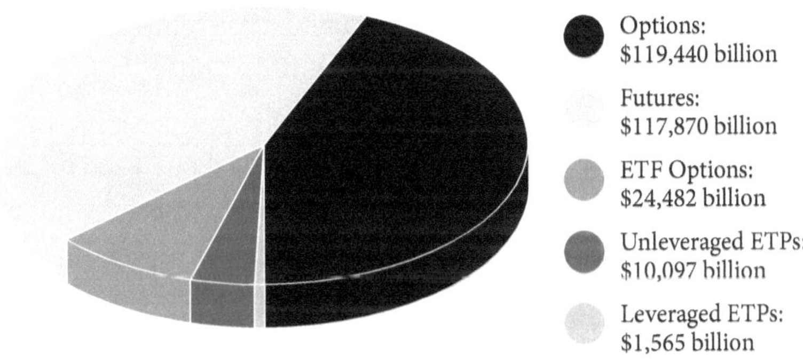

The $278-Trillion S&P 500 Trading Ecosystem

Diagram 3-2

Measuring S&P 500 Returns

The returns of the S&P 500 can be measured in two ways:

1. **Price alone.**
   This represents the % change in the index from one date to the next (daily, weekly, monthly, quarterly, etc.). The S&P 500 is a price index that is calculated using a specific methodology that we'll cover later. The index was 6,846 on December 31, 2025.

2. **Total return.**
   This reflects the change in price plus it assumes that any issued dividends were immediately reinvested in the S&P 500 to purchase more of the index.

Historically, the difference between price return and total return is about 2% per year.[16] It was more in the early years of the index, but is less now as buybacks have increased. As highlighted in the Introduction to this book, reinvested dividends contributed about 1.5% to the 2025 total return.

If the price return is around 8% and the dividend return is around 2%, then the total annual return is around 10%. This does not mean the index goes up 10% each year. It fluctuates, and 10% is the average annual return.[17]

Over the last 20 years, the average total return is about 11%, but if you go all the way back to the launch of the index, it is lower.[18] The selection methodology and calculation has changed over time, but the last 20 years best reflects the methodology and calculation in place today.

Think of the index as a triangle with the price # (value) at the top. The price rests on many separate building blocks or layers. These layers include:

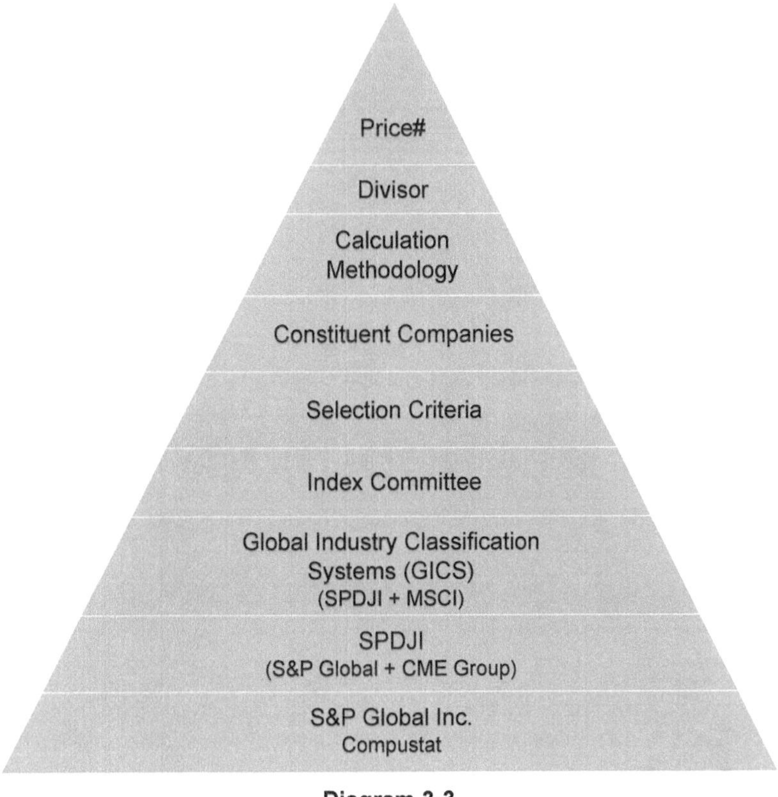

Diagram 3-3

The following chapters will cover all of the layers of the S&P 500 in detail to paint a picture of how the S&P 500 works.

CHAPTER 4

ELIGIBILITY CRITERIA AND CONSTITUENT SELECTION METHODOLOGY

The purpose of the S&P 500 is to measure the health and productive output of the U.S. economy, as represented by the performance of the large-cap segment of the United States equity market. It is deliberately structured to serve as a robust proxy for the overall U.S. equity market, offering a comprehensive snapshot of this critical asset class. The Index Committee, which oversees the S&P 500, endeavors to ensure that the index remains a leading indicator of U.S. equities. This involves a continuous effort to accurately reflect the risk and return characteristics of the broader large-cap universe on an ongoing basis.

These objectives inform every aspect of the index's

methodology, starting with the initial selection of constituent companies. The process of selecting companies for inclusion in the S&P 500 is governed by a stringent set of quantitative and qualitative eligibility criteria designed to ensure the index comprises leading, investable U.S. companies. These criteria act as the foundational pillars upon which the index's integrity and representativeness are built.

To be eligible for inclusion, a company must be part of the S&P Total Market Index, be a U.S.-domiciled company and trade on a major U.S. exchange. It must also satisfy the U.S. Securities Exchange Act's periodic reporting obligations by filing forms for domestic issuers, such as, but not limited to: Form 10-K annual reports, Form 10-Q quarterly reports, and Form 8-K current reports. The company must be a corporation and must issue common stock.

A primary screening criterion for S&P 500 inclusion is market capitalization. To be considered for addition, a company must meet a minimum market capitalization threshold. According to the October 2025 SPDJI Index Methodology, this threshold is set at US $22.7 billion or greater. This figure is subject to periodic review and adjustment by SPDJI to reflect prevailing market conditions and growth; for example, the threshold was US $20.5 billion immediately prior to the October 2025 update.[19] The minimum threshold is set to capture the 85th percentile of market capitalization of the S&P Total Market Index. This threshold is reviewed each calendar quarter. As at October 2025, the mid-cap threshold was $8.0–$22.7 billion and captured the 85th to 93rd percentile, and the small-cap threshold was $1.2–$8.0 billion and captured the 93rd to 99th percentile.

Beyond the total company market capitalization, there is

an additional requirement related to the investable portion of the company's value. The security-level float-adjusted market capitalization (FMC) must be at least 50% of the respective index's total company-level minimum market capitalization threshold. It is crucial to note that these market capitalization eligibility criteria are specifically for addition to the index. An existing constituent that subsequently falls below these thresholds is not automatically removed unless ongoing conditions warrant such an index change. This asymmetry in application promotes index stability and helps to minimize unnecessary turnover, which can be costly for index-tracking investment products.

The S&P 500 is designed to reflect the U.S. equity market. Therefore, a company must qualify as a U.S. company to be eligible for inclusion. The determination of U.S. company status involves several factors. A key requirement is that the company must have its primary listing on an eligible U.S. stock exchange, such as the New York Stock Exchange (including NYSE Arca or NYSE American), Nasdaq (Nasdaq Global Select Market or Nasdaq Capital Market), or Cboe BZX.

Other considerations include the company's SEC filing status (typically filing 10-K annual reports), and the geographical distribution of its fixed assets and revenues, with a plurality ideally situated in the U.S. In cases of ambiguity, the location of fixed assets generally takes precedence, and revenue location is used if asset information is incomplete. The Index Committee retains the authority to make the final determination of domicile eligibility. It may consider other relevant factors, including the location of operational headquarters, the composition of its officers, directors, and employees, investor perception, and the company's incorporation status. Notably, companies that may be registered for tax purposes in what are sometimes termed "domiciles of convenience" are generally still considered U.S. companies if other substantive ties to the U.S. are evident. This discretionary power allows the Committee to navigate the complexities of increasingly globalized corporate structures while upholding the index's US focus.

High liquidity is a non-negotiable prerequisite for S&P 500 constituents. This ensures that the index components can be bought and sold by large institutional investors without causing undue price distortions, a critical feature for the efficient replication of the index by passive investment vehicles. Liquidity is assessed through several metrics. There is a minimum trading volume requirement: a stock must have traded a minimum of 250,000 shares in each of the six months preceding the evaluation date. A key measure is the ratio of annual dollar value traded to float-adjusted market capitalization. For addition to the S&P Composite 1500 (which includes the S&P 500), the float-adjusted liquidity ratio (FALR) must be greater than or equal to 0.75 at the time of addition. So, at least 75% of the float-adjusted value of the company must trade hands each year.

In addition to size and liquidity, companies must demonstrate financial viability to qualify for the S&P 500. This criterion introduces a qualitative layer, aiming to ensure the inclusion of established, profitable enterprises. Specifically, the sum of a company's most recent four consecutive quarters' Generally Accepted Accounting Principles (GAAP) earnings (defined as net income excluding discontinued operations) must be positive. Additionally, the GAAP earnings for the single most recent quarter must also be positive. For Equity Real Estate Investment Trusts (REITs), financial viability assessment may also consider Funds From Operations (FFO), if reported, alongside or in lieu of GAAP earnings.

A significant portion of a company's shares must be available for public trading. This is quantified by the Investable Weight Factor (IWF), which must be at least 0.10 for the S&P Composite 1500 constituents, including those in the S&P 500. The IWF represents the percentage of a company's total outstanding shares that are freely available to public investors, thereby excluding shares that are closely held by insiders, controlling shareholders, governments, or other corporations. This requirement ensures that the index accurately reflects the market segment accessible to the investing public and that constituent weights are not skewed by large, illiquid blocks of stock.

While not a rigid quantitative criterion in the same vein as market capitalization or liquidity thresholds, sector balance is an important consideration in the constituent selection process. The Index Committee analyzes the weight of each Global Industry Classification Standard (GICS) sector within the S&P 500 and compares it to that sector's weight in the broader S&P Total Market Index, specifically within the relevant large-cap range. This qualitative assessment helps to ensure that the S&P 500 maintains its character as a diversified proxy for the U.S. large-cap market and avoids undue concentration in any particular sector. All companies within SPDJI are classified according to GICS, providing a consistent and hierarchical framework for analysis.

To maintain the index's focus on common equity of operating companies and ensure a degree of homogeneity among its constituents, certain types of securities and organizational structures are explicitly ineligible for inclusion. These exclusions typically encompass limited partnerships (LPs), master limited partnerships (MLPs) and their investment trust units, Over-the-Counter (OTC) Bulletin Board issues, closed-end funds, exchange-traded funds (ETFs), exchange-traded notes (ETNs), royalty trusts, tracking stocks, preferred stock, unit trusts, and equity warrants.

There is also a seasoning requirement. Specific rules apply to companies that have recently undergone an Initial Public Offering (IPO) or emerged from bankruptcy. Generally, IPOs are required to have been traded on an eligible U.S. exchange for a minimum of 12 months before they can be considered for addition to an S&P index like the S&P 500. There is no provision to "fast track" entry into the S&P Composite 1500 for IPOs. Similarly, companies emerging from bankruptcy proceedings typically must also trade on an eligible exchange for at least 12 months before being considered for inclusion in the S&P Composite 1500. This "seasoning" period allows for a period of price discovery and market stabilization, ensuring that newly considered companies have a more established trading history and valuation, thereby reducing the risk of incorporating overly volatile or unproven entities into the benchmark.

The interplay of these quantitative rules and qualitative overlays is a defining characteristic of the S&P 500's eligibility framework. While hard data on market cap, trading volume, and earnings provide the initial screens, the Index Committee's judgment on factors like "sector balance" or the nuanced determination of "U.S. company" status is critical. This hybrid approach allows the index to adapt to a dynamic market environment but also underscores the importance of transparent governance over how much discretion is exercised.

These stringent eligibility criteria effectively create a significant barrier to entry for companies aspiring to S&P 500 inclusion. Given that membership is often viewed as a hallmark of corporate success and can trigger substantial investor demand due to the proliferation of index-tracking funds, these rules can indirectly influence corporate behavior. Companies approaching the required thresholds might be incentivized to manage their financial reporting, corporate structure, or investor relations strategies in a manner that enhances their eligibility. Furthermore, the principle that eligibility criteria are primarily for addition to the index, with existing members not facing automatic removal for minor deviations, contributes to a degree of "stickiness" in the index's composition. This policy is designed to reduce unnecessary turnover, thereby lowering transaction costs for funds that replicate the index. However, it also implies that the index might, at times, include companies that would not qualify based on the current eligibility criteria, representing a deliberate trade-off between precise, moment-in-time representation and the practicalities of investability and cost-efficiency.

The Index Committee

The integrity and relevance of the S&P 500 are significantly shaped by the S&P Dow Jones Index Committee. This body acts as the steward of the index, responsible for interpreting and applying the methodology, making decisions on constituent changes, and ensuring the index continues to meet its overarching objectives. S&P's U.S. indices, which include the flagship S&P 500, are overseen and maintained by the Index Committee. A critical aspect of its composition is that all voting members are full-time professional staff members of SPDJI. To maintain objectivity and prevent potential conflicts of interest, these members are senior individuals who do not have commercial responsibilities within the organization. The Committee typically convenes on a monthly basis to conduct its reviews and make decisions, although it can meet more frequently if market conditions or specific events necessitate.

The mandate of the Index Committee is comprehensive. Its overarching goal is to ensure that the S&P 500 remains a premier, leading indicator of the U.S. large-cap equities. This involves continuously monitoring the market to ensure the index accurately reflects its risk and return characteristics, overseeing constituent liquidity to maintain investability, and striving to minimize unnecessary turnover in the index's composition.

While the S&P methodology is fundamentally rules-based, providing a clear framework for index construction and maintenance, the Index Committee is vested with a degree of discretion and the ability to exercise expert judgment. This human element is particularly crucial when addressing exceptional or unforeseen circumstances that may not be explicitly covered by the established methodology or SPDJI policies.

The Committee may apply its discretion in various situations, such as to avoid excessive index turnover that could be disruptive and costly for tracking funds, to prevent unnecessary changes driven by transient market conditions, to mitigate potential market disruption from index adjustments, or to enhance the overall replicability and investability of the index. Ultimately, the Index Committee reserves the right to make exceptions to the standard application of the methodology if deemed necessary to ensure that the index continues to achieve its stated objectives. This careful balance between adherence to rules and the application of informed judgement allows the S&P 500 to adapt to an ever-evolving market landscape while maintaining its credibility.

The Committee's capacity for discretion effectively positions it as a risk mitigation function. In a complex and dynamic financial world, a rigid, purely mechanical application of rules could, in certain scenarios, lead to undesirable outcomes such as excessive churn, increased transaction costs for the multitude of funds tracking the index, or the inclusion or exclusion of companies based on short-lived technicalities rather than sustained market leadership or viability. The Committee's judgment acts as a crucial buffer, aiming for a more stable, representative, and economically sensible index over the long term.

The Index Committee conducts regular reviews of several key areas. During its meetings, the Committee assesses pending corporate actions that may affect index constituents, analyzes statistical data comparing the index's composition to the broader market, evaluates companies that are being considered as candidates for addition or removal, and discusses any significant market events that could have implications for the index.

Due to the highly market-sensitive nature of potential index changes, the deliberations within the Index Committee are kept confidential to prevent premature disclosure and potential market manipulation. However, once decisions on changes to the index's composition (such as additions or deletions of companies) are made, SPDJI announces these changes publicly. Typically, such announcements are made with at least three business days' advance notice before the changes become effective, although the Committee retains the discretion to provide less notice if circumstances warrant.

Regarding changes to the index methodology itself, SPDJI has established processes that may include public consultation, particularly for alterations deemed material. A material methodology change is defined as one that alters the index objective or modifies the methodology in such a way that affects the likelihood of the index achieving its objective, such as a change to the rule determining the eligible universe, constituent selection, or weighting. Furthermore, SPDJI maintains internal records documenting instances where expert judgment has been applied, along with the rationale for such decisions.

This operational framework highlights a careful balancing act between the need for confidentiality during sensitive deliberations and the commitment to transparency required by the market. While the specific discussions leading to constituent changes remain private, the extensive publication of methodology documents and the potential for public input on significant methodology revisions provide a degree of openness. The mandated advance notice period for implemented changes serves as a critical bridge, offering market participants a window to prepare and adjust without compromising the integrity of the decision-making process itself.

The structured management of information flow is a key element of the S&P 500's governance. The authority of the Index Committee to revise the index policy and the established procedures for methodology changes underscore that the S&P 500 methodology is not a static set of rules. Instead, it functions as a "living document", evolving under the Committee's stewardship to adapt to transformations in market structures, the emergence of new financial instruments, and shifts in economic conditions. This inherent adaptability, formalized by at least an annual review of the methodology, is essential for the index to maintain its long-term relevance and utility as a leading market benchmark.

Constituent Changes

A distinguishing feature of the S&P 500's maintenance is its approach to constituent changes. Unlike many indices that have fixed, scheduled reconstitution dates where the entire list of companies is reviewed for additions and deletions, the S&P 500 does not follow such a rigid schedule for these types of changes. Instead, alterations to the index's roster of companies—additions and deletions—are made on an "as-needed" basis. These changes are typically triggered by significant corporate actions such as mergers, acquisitions, or bankruptcies, or by market developments that cause a company to no longer meet eligibility criteria or another company to become a compelling candidate for inclusion. Such adjustments can, therefore, occur at any time throughout the year. These changes are effectively the buy and sell decisions of the Index Committee. The fund provider that is tracking the index, e.g., Vanguard for VFIAX or VOO, will buy the stock of a company when it is added and sell the stock of a company when it is removed.

However, it is important to distinguish this "as-needed" approach for constituent changes from other types of index adjustments. The S&P 500 does undergo a quarterly rebalancing cycle, typically on the third Friday of March, June, September, and December. These quarterly events are primarily focused on updating the share counts of existing constituents to reflect recent issuances or buybacks, reviewing and adjusting Investable Weight Factors (IWFs), and implementing weight adjustments in related S&P 500 indices that have scheduled rebalancing, such as the S&P 500 Equal Weight Index or style indices.

This dual-track approach—"as-needed" for constituent changes and quarterly for share/IWF updates—allows the S&P

500 to be highly responsive to major, market-altering events while maintaining a degree of operational predictability for routine adjustments. The "as-needed" philosophy for additions and deletions ensures that the index can promptly reflect the impact of significant corporate transformations, thereby preserving its representativeness. However, this responsiveness also introduces an element of unpredictability for market participants compared to indices with strictly scheduled reconstitutions. Investment managers tracking the S&P 500 must maintain operational readiness to implement off-cycle trades, which can have implications for trading strategies and transaction costs.When the Index Committee determines that a change in the S&P 500's composition is warranted, such additions or deletions are publicly announced with at least three business days' advance notice before the changes take effect. This notice period allows market participants, particularly index-tracking funds, to prepare for necessary trades.

A company will be deleted from the index if it is involved in a merger, acquisition, or significant corporate restructuring that results in it no longer meeting the established eligibility criteria. Similarly, if a company substantially violates one or more of the core eligibility criteria on an ongoing basis, the Index Committee may decide to remove it. Delisting from an eligible exchange and moving to trade on the pink sheets or the OTC Bulletin Board will also trigger removal.

To maintain index quality and prevent the rapid cycling of companies in and out of the benchmark, any company that is removed from the S&P 500 (whether due to M&A, discretionary decisions, bankruptcy, or exchange delistings) must typically wait a minimum of one year from its removal date before it can be screened again for eligibility and potential re-addition. Throughout this process, the Index Committee aims to minimize unnecessary turnover in the index, balancing the need for accurate representation with the practical considerations of index tracking.

Corporate actions are frequent occurrences in the life of public companies and can have significant implications for their status within the S&P 500 and for the index itself. SPDJI has established policies and practices to handle these events consistently.

Mergers and acquisitions (M&A) are primary drivers of changes in the S&P 500's composition. When an S&P 500 constituent is acquired or merges with another company, it is typically deleted from the index. This removal usually occurs on or around the target company's expected delisting date or the date the M&A event is deemed unconditional (i.e., all required approvals are received and all conditions for completion are met).

If the acquiring company is not already an S&P 500 constituent, it may be considered for addition if it meets the standard eligibility criteria. In certain circumstances, particularly if the acquiring company issues stock to the target company's shareholders as part of the transaction, the Index Committee may exercise discretion to add the acquirer even if it does not perfectly meet all eligibility criteria. This can help to mitigate index turnover and maintain the index's representativeness of the newly formed entity's market presence.

When an S&P 500 constituent company spins off a part of its business into a new, publicly traded entity, specific rules govern the treatment of the spun-off company. These newly created entities do not necessarily need to meet all the standard "outside addition" criteria (like the 12-month trading history) to be included in an S&P Composite 1500 index, provided they are U.S.- domiciled. The Index Committee evaluates the spin-off, often using when-issued prices if available, and may decide to retain the spin-off company in the parent stock's index (e.g. S&P 500) if the Committee determines its total market capitalization is representative of that index.

If an S&P 500 constituent files for bankruptcy protection, it may be deleted from the index at the discretion of the Index Committee, particularly if it substantially violates the ongoing eligibility criteria as a result of the bankruptcy. If a company's stock is delisted from its primary exchange and moves to the pink sheets or the OTC Bulletin Board—often a consequence of severe financial distress or bankruptcy—it is removed from the index. Securities removed due to delisting (non-bankruptcy) may be removed at the OTC or pink sheet price if available, or at a zero price if no such price is available. Companies that successfully emerge from bankruptcy proceedings and wish to be reconsidered for S&P 1500 inclusion must typically trade on an eligible U.S. exchange for at least 12 months post-emergence before being screened. These rules ensure that the index does not continue to carry stocks that are no longer viable or fail to meet basic listing and trading standards, while the waiting period post-emergence ensures a degree of stability and proven market viability before reconsideration.

Common S&P 500 Company Actions

<u>Stock Splits:</u>
When a company undergoes a stock split (e.g. 2-for-1), the number of its shares in the index is multiplied by the split factor, and its stock price is correspondingly divided by the same factor.

This adjustment ensures that the company's float-adjusted market capitalization, and therefore its weight in the index, remains unchanged immediately following the split. Share counts for all constituents are formally reviewed and updated on a quarterly basis.

<u>Share Repurchases and Issuance:</u>
These actions alter a company's number of outstanding shares and consequently, its float-adjusted market capitalization. The S&P U.S. Indices' methodology indicates that share counts are updated quarterly to reflect these changes.

<u>Regular Dividends:</u>
The commonly quoted S&P 500 Index level is a "price return" index, which means it does not account for the reinvestment of cash dividends paid by constituent companies. However, SPDJI also calculates and disseminates Total Return (TR) versions of the index (e.g., the S&P 500 Total Return Index, ticker SPTR), which do include the impact of reinvested dividends. Gross Total Return versions reinvest regular cash dividends on the ex-dividend date without deducting withholding taxes, while Net Total Return versions reinvest dividends after accounting for applicable withholding taxes.

<u>Special Dividends:</u>
Special or extraordinary cash dividends are treated differently from regular dividends. Generally, these are not included as dividend points in SPDJI's annual dividend indices. Instead, for the price return version of the S&P 500, a special dividend typically results in an adjustment to the index divisor. This divisor adjustment is made to neutralize the impact of the large,

one-off payout on the index level, preventing an artificial drop in the index that would otherwise occur due to the ex-dividend price decline of the paying company's stock.

<u>Rights Issues:</u>
When a company conducts a rights issue (offering existing shareholders the right to buy additional shares at a specified price), index adjustments are typically made to maintain the index's continuity. For market capitalization-weighted indices, the general principle is to adjust for the theoretical value of the right to ensure that the company's weight in the index is not artificially distorted by the mechanical price drop on the ex-rights date. SPDJI's Corporate Actions Policies provide detailed definitions and treatment guidelines for various types of rights offerings, including renounceable, non-renounceable, and accelerated rights offerings. These adjustments aim to ensure the index continues to accurately reflect the aggregate market value of its constituents.

The diverse and often complex nature of these corporate actions means that a simple, rigid rulebook cannot anticipate every nuance. The Index Committee's role in interpreting how these events affect eligibility, weighting, and overall index continuity is therefore paramount. Decisions regarding, for example, the treatment of a particularly complex spin-off or a merger involving a non-constituent company require careful judgment to ensure the index's objectives are consistently upheld. This underscores that index maintenance, while grounded in clear policies, is not a purely algorithmic process and often requires expert human oversight.

Furthermore, the changes made to the S&P 500's composition, whether additions or deletions, are significant events for the companies involved and the broader market. These changes often lead to substantial increases (for additions) or decreases (for deletions) in trading volume and can cause short-term price movements in the affected stocks as index-tracking funds rebalance their portfolios to align with the updated index. This "index effect" highlights the tangible real-world impact of the S&P 500 methodology and its application. The Index Committee's stated aim of minimizing unnecessary turnover and the practice of providing advance notice of changes demonstrate an awareness of these market impacts and an attempt to manage them responsibly.

In 2024, there were 32 companies that cycled through the S&P 500, 16 in and 16 out. In 2025, there were 38 companies that cycled through, 19 in and 19 out.[20] Some are new companies like Robinhood and AppLovin that are replacing companies moving down to the SmallCap 600 Index, like CarMax and Caesars Entertainment. Others are being spun out of larger companies to stand alone, like Solstice Advanced Materials and Qnity Electronics, while others have been acquired and are being removed, like Interpublic Group or Walgreens Boots Alliance.

The Premier U.S. Equity Benchmark

The S&P 500's enduring status as the premier U.S. equity benchmark is a testament to a meticulously crafted methodology and a governance framework designed to uphold its integrity, representativeness, and investability. Its selection criteria and maintenance procedures reflect a sophisticated understanding of market dynamics and investor needs.

The entire S&P 500 methodology, from its stringent multifaceted eligibility criteria— encompassing market capitalization, U.S. domicile, liquidity, financial viability, and public float—to its foundational float-adjusted market capitalization weighting scheme, demonstrates a deep-seated commitment to accurately representing the U.S. large-cap equity market. Simultaneously, the active oversight provided by the S&P Dow Jones Index Committee ensures that the index remains a practical, efficient, and replicable tool for a global investor base. The carefully calibrated balance between clearly defined, objective rules and the capacity for discretionary judgment by the Committee is pivotal. This allows the index to adapt to unique market situations or company-specific events that might not be perfectly captured by a purely algorithmic approach, thereby enhancing both its representativeness and its utility as an investment benchmark.

The S&P 500 is not a static construct. It is a dynamic entity that evolves in tandem with the financial markets it seeks to measure. This adaptability is evidenced by periodic updates to its eligibility criteria, such as the adjustments to market capitalization thresholds to reflect market growth and inflation. Furthermore, the ongoing review of index policies and methodologies by the Index Committee, coupled with established procedures for implementing methodology changes (which may include public consultation for material alterations), underscores its capacity for evolution. This commitment to periodic refinement and adaptation ensures that the S&P 500 maintains its relevance and continues to serve as an accurate barometer of U.S. large-cap equities amidst changing market structures, emerging investment trends, and evolving economic conditions.

The governance structure of the S&P 500, embodied by the Index Committee and its operational policies, reflects broader principles of sound governance within financial markets. The emphasis on the objectivity of committee members (senior, non-commercial staff), the structured management of market-sensitive information, the transparency provided through public methodology documents and announcements of changes, and adherence to relevant regulatory standards and recognized industry best practices all contribute to the index's widespread credibility and adoption.[21]

A comprehensive understanding of the S&P 500's selection criteria and its detailed operational methodology is of paramount importance for a wide spectrum of market participants. For institutional and individual investors who utilize the S&P 500 as a critical benchmark for performance measurement, a nuanced appreciation of its construction rules is essential for contextualizing returns and making informed asset allocation decisions. For the vast number of investors who allocate capital to S&P 500-tracking products, such as ETFs and index funds, knowledge of how companies are selected, weighted, and maintained within the index provides clarity on the underlying exposures of their investments.

The subtleties of the index's construction and maintenance—particularly the pivotal role of the Index Committee, its application of discretion, and the precise mechanisms for handling diverse corporate actions—have tangible and often significant impacts on portfolio performance, trading dynamics, and the valuation of individual securities. The enduring challenge for SPDJI is to continually balance the needs of passive replication, which favors stability and predictability, with the necessity of active, expert oversight to ensure the index's long-term integrity and relevance. This careful stewardship, navigating the inherent duality of being a benchmark for passive strategies while requiring active judgment in its upkeep, will be crucial for the S&P 500's continued success as a leading global financial benchmark.

CHAPTER 5

CALCULATION METHODOLOGY

The Standard Statistics Bureau was founded by Luther Lee Blake in 1906. His venture aimed to provide financial information on non-railroad companies, a burgeoning sector of the American economy that was under-covered by existing financial services, which were heavily focused on the dominant railroad industry. This focus on a broader industrial base was a precursor to the philosophy that would later guide the S&P 500. In 1923, Standard Statistics developed its first stock market index, a composite of 233 U.S. companies, which was computed using a market-weighted average on a weekly basis. This was one of the first major attempts to systematically track a wide cross-section of the U.S. market, moving beyond the narrow focus of the DJIA.

A more direct ancestor of the modern S&P 500 emerged in 1926. In that year, Standard Statistics created a 90-stock

"Composite Price Index". This index was more structured, comprising 50 industrial, 20 railroad, and 20 utility stocks, reflecting the key economic pillars of the time. A critical advancement occurred in 1928 when the calculation of this 90-stock index became a daily event. This transition to a daily computation provided a much more timely and useful pulse of market activity, establishing a new standard for market indicators and laying the groundwork for the high-frequency calculations that would follow decades later. The S&P 500 lists the first value date as January 3, 1928.

The most significant and enduring innovation of these early indices was their calculation methodology. From its very first index in 1923, Standard Statistics employed a capitalization-weighted approach, which it termed a "base-weighted aggregate technique". This method calculates an index's value by weighing each constituent stock according to its total market value—the stock's price multiplied by its number of shares outstanding.

This choice represented a fundamental philosophical departure from the price-weighted methodology of the DJIA. In a price-weighted index like the Dow, a stock with a high per-share price has more influence than a stock with a low per-share price, regardless of the company's overall economic significance. The capitalization-weighted approach, by contrast, posits that a company's total market value is the most accurate reflection of its importance to the overall economy and market. This decision, made in the 1920s, established the core principle that has defined the S&P 500 for nearly a century: economic scale, not share price, determines a company's weight in the benchmark. The formula is a modification of a Laspeyres index, where the numerator becomes a measure of current market value and the denominator is replaced by a divisor that sets the base value. This is similar to how CPI is calculated, but instead of measuring how the price of a basket of goods changes over time, the S&P 500 measures how the value of a basket of companies changes over time.

Prior to 1957, the S&P Composite was a 480-stock Index that was calculated once a week on Wednesdays. The base year period for the S&P Composite was intentionally chosen to be an average of the three-year period from 1941 to 1943, using a base of 10. The base from the early '40s was carried over to the S&P 500. As highlighted earlier in the book, trading began at 44.22 on opening day, and stood at 6,846 at the end of 2025.

The purpose of a base period is to provide a reference point for the market. From 1941 to 1943, the U.S. industrial economy was operating at maximum capacity due to World War II. Rather than choosing a single week or year, which could be skewed by a sudden spike or crash, S&P used the average of weekly group values across three years. This smoothed out short-term volatility and provided a more reliable statistical floor. This also aligned with the corporate merger between Standard Statistics Company and Poor's Publishing, effectively allowing them to create a consistent methodology to replace the various older indexes that each company used. By setting the base year after the merger, they effectively relaunched the index as the new standard.

The index of 1955 was a statement of "How much is the current total market value of these 480 companies worth compared to the average total value of 1941 to 1943?" The same base period and base value of 10 are still used today, so the S&P 500's current level represents its growth relative to the original World War II era base period.

The Capitalization Weighting Formula

While the concept of tracking 500 stocks is simple, the calculation that produces the final index level is a sophisticated process designed to ensure accuracy, consistency, and continuity over time. The two core components of the engine are the capitalization-weighting formula and the index divisor.

The S&P 500 has always been a capitalization-weighted index. The fundamental formula for calculating the index level is the sum of the market capitalizations of all constituent companies, divided by the index divisor. The formula can be expressed as:

$$\text{Index Level} = \frac{\sum_{i=1}^{N} (P_i \times Q_i)}{\text{the divisor}}$$

Where:
- P_i is the current price of stock i.
- Q_i is the number of shares for stock i used in the calculation. Initially, this was the total number of shares outstanding; it was later modified to be the number of publicly available (float-adjusted) shares.
- N is the number of companies in the index (approximately 500).

(Said another way: you take the stock price of a company and multiply it by the number of outstanding shares (later modified to the number of shares that the general public can buy—this is what float-adjusted means). This gets you the float-adjusted, capitalization-weighted market value of that company at that moment in time. You do this for every company in the index and add all of the values together to get the total adjusted value of all companies in the index, then divide that by a proprietary number called the divisor that is designed to maintain the consistency and stability of the index.)

The Divisor:
The Unseen Hand Ensuring Index Continuity

While the numerator of the formula represents the adjusted market value of the index, the divisor is the crucial, yet often misunderstood, component that makes the index a coherent and continuous benchmark. The divisor is a proprietary and arbitrary number maintained by SPDJI that serves two essential functions.

Scaling:
The aggregate market capitalization of the 500 companies in the index is an immense number, currently in the tens of trillions of dollars. Reporting this unwieldy figure would be impractical. The divisor scales this massive value down to a more manageable and easily reportable number such as 7,000.

Maintaining Continuity:
This is the divisor's most critical role. The value of a benchmark must only reflect genuine market movements (i.e., changes in stock prices). It should not be distorted by corporate actions or changes to the index's composition. The divisor is the mechanism that neutralizes these non-market events.

Any corporate or index event that alters the total market value of the numerator without being a result of pure stock price movement requires a corresponding adjustment to the divisor. Such events include:

- Adding or deleting a company from the index.
- A constituent company issuing new shares or repurchasing its own stock.
- Stock splits, reverse stock splits, and stock dividends.
- Special, non-recurring cash dividends.
- Spinoffs of a subsidiary into a new company.
- Changes to a stock's Investable Weight Factor (IWF) due to float adjustments.

The adjustment process ensures that the index value remains constant immediately before and after the event, preserving the continuity of the time series. The conceptual calculation for an adjustment is as follows:

New Divisor = Old Divisor x (post-event market value/pre-event market value)

By adjusting the divisor, S&P ensures that if the index closes at 4,500.50 on one day, and a company is replaced overnight, the index will still open at 4,500.50 the next morning, assuming no other stock prices have changed. This constant, behind-the-scenes maintenance transforms a simple valuation into a scientifically valid historical record, making the divisor the true guardian of the index's integrity.

Compustat Data

The quantitative analysis performed by the Index Committee and the historical calculation of the index itself would be impossible without a clean, reliable, and standardized source of financial data. For most of the S&P 500's history, that data backbone has been Compustat.

Launched by Standard & Poor's in 1962, Compustat was a revolutionary product for its time. It is a comprehensive database containing decades of fundamental financial and market data for thousands of global companies, with some annual data stretching back to 1950. In the 1960s, this data was distributed on magnetic tapes for use in mainframe computers.

Compustat's true innovation was not just data aggregation, but data standardization. Corporate financial reports are often inconsistent in their presentation. Compustat analysts review company filings and adjust line items to conform to a standardized format, allowing for accurate, apples-to-apples comparisons between companies and across time. This service was indispensable for the development of large-scale quantitative financial analysis and academic research. For decades, Compustat was the primary data source for S&P's own index maintenance and for countless research papers analyzing the market.

Today, the calculation and dissemination of the S&P 500 is a high-technology operation. While SPDJI manages the methodology and governance, it relies on a network of partners. High-speed data providers feed real-time price information from exchanges. Specialized calculation agents run the index formulas on powerful servers. And global dissemination partners like Reuters ensure that the updated index value reaches terminals, websites, and television screens around the world within milliseconds of its calculation. This intricate infrastructure ensures the index can serve its modern role as a near-instantaneous benchmark for global markets.

The Evolution of the Methodology

The S&P 500's calculation methodology has continuously evolved since its creation in 1957. It has been driven by technological advancements that allowed for greater speed and precision, structural realignments to better reflect the changing U.S. economy, and a fundamental rethinking of market capitalization itself in response to the rise of passive investing.

The hourly calculations enabled by Melpar, Inc. in 1957 were just the beginning of a relentless march toward real-time data. In 1962, Ultronic Systems became the compiler for the S&P indices, indicating an ongoing specialization in the computational power required for index maintenance.

A significant leap occurred in 1986 when the index value began to be calculated and disseminated by Reuters every 15 seconds. This represented a massive increase in data frequency from the minute-by-minute updates that had been the standard just prior. This move to near-real-time calculations was not just a technical curiosity; it was a critical development that supported the explosive growth of the financial derivatives market. The Chicago Mercantile Exchange (CME) had begun trading futures contracts based on the S&P 500 in 1982, followed by the Chicago Board Options Exchange (CBOE) launching options on the index in 1983. These instruments required a constantly updated, reliable underlying index value to function. The introduction of the hugely popular S&P E-mini futures contract by CME in 1997 further democratized access to trading the index and cemented the need for high-frequency, trustworthy data.

The most significant methodological change to the S&P 500 since its inception occurred in 2005 with the transition to a public float-adjusted capitalization weighting. The rationale for this monumental shift was directly tied to the success of the index itself and the rise of passive investing. By the early 2000s, trillions of dollars in assets held by index funds and exchange-traded funds (ETFs) were benchmarked to the S&P 500. These funds operate by attempting to replicate the index's holdings in their exact proportions. Under the total market capitalization system, a fund was required to buy shares proportional to a company's total shares outstanding. However, a significant portion of shares in many companies is often held by strategic investors—such as founding families, governments, or other corporations—and is not available for public trading.

This created a mismatch between the index's theoretical construction and the practical reality of the market. Index funds were forced to try to buy shares that were not on the open market, creating artificial price pressure and liquidity problems, particularly for companies with a small "free float". This "index effect", where the act of being included in the index distorts a stock's price, necessitated a change.

The transition to a float-adjusted methodology was implemented in phases during 2005 and became fully effective on September 16, 2005. The calculation of each company's market cap was modified to exclude restricted shares. S&P implements this by assigning each company an Investable Weight Factor (IWF), which represents the percentage of total shares that are available for public trading. The formula for a company's weight thus became:

Float-Adjusted Market Cap = Share Price x Total Shares Outstanding x IWF

This change made the S&P 500 a more accurate and investable benchmark, as it now reflects the market capitalization that is actually accessible to public investors. While the adjustment improved overall liquidity and reduced market distortions, it also subtly changed the economic characteristics of the index by reducing the weight of companies with large, closely held blocks of stock. This evolution marked a critical turning point, acknowledging that the S&P 500 was no longer just a passive observer of the market, but an active participant whose own size and structure could influence market behavior. This would make historic comparisons starting on October 1, 2005, and later, most representative of the current index methodology.

The history of the S&P 500's calculation methodology is far more than a series of technical adjustments. It is a narrative that mirrors the evolution of the American economy, the relentless progress of technology, and the maturation of financial theory. From its conceptual birth in the 1920s as a capitalization-weighted alternative to its price-weighted peers, the index was founded on a distinct philosophy: that a company's economic scale is the true measure of its market significance. This foundational principle has endured for a century.

The journey from the 90-stock daily index of 1928 to the 500-stock, float-adjusted, high-frequency benchmark of today reveals a process of constant adaptation. The 1957 launch was a watershed moment, but one made possible only by the computational power of early mainframes and the technical know-how supplied by Melpar, Inc. The subsequent increase in calculation speed, from hourly to every 15 seconds, was driven by the demands of a burgeoning derivatives market that relied on the index as its underlying asset.

Perhaps the most profound evolution was the 2005 shift to free-float adjustment. This change marked the moment the index could no longer be seen as a purely passive observer of the market. The immense growth of passive investing, an industry the S&P 500 itself helped create, generated a powerful feedback loop. The index's own construction began to influence market dynamics, forcing its stewards to alter the methodology to better reflect the investable reality. This event solidified the S&P 500's role not just as a barometer, but as an integral and influential component of the market's structure.

CHAPTER 6

THE S&P 500'S ROLE IN FINANCIAL MARKETS

The S&P 500's pervasiveness extends beyond being a simple market barometer; it forms the underlying basis for numerous derivative financial products, and is a key indicator of broader economic sentiment and investor confidence. Such widespread integration necessitates significant engagement from regulatory and governmental entities tasked with maintaining market stability and investor protection.

Market-Wide Circuit Breakers (MWCBs)

The most direct and visible way the S&P 500 influences regulatory action is through pre-defined mechanisms designed to curb extreme market volatility. These primarily take the form of market-wide and single-security circuit breakers, alongside regulatory responses to the behavior of financial products indexed to the S&P 500.

Stock market circuit breakers are regulatory measures that temporarily halt trading on an exchange during periods of excessive volatility or significant market declines. Functioning as emergency brakes for the financial markets, the primary objective is to curb panic selling, provide a "time out" for the market to regroup, and allow for the orderly dissemination of information. By interrupting trading, these mechanisms aim to manage liquidity and promote a more rational trading environment.

In essence, circuit breakers are designed to prevent market meltdowns by offering a cooling-off period for investors to reassess prevailing conditions and make more informed decisions. The implementation of circuit breakers extends beyond the immediate concern of preventing losses for individual investors; it is fundamentally about safeguarding the stability and integrity of the entire financial market system. Unchecked panic selling can lead to a cascading effect, where falling prices trigger further sales, potentially detaching market valuations from fundamental economic realities.

Such a scenario can have far-reaching systemic implications impacting credit markets, business investment, and overall economic confidence. The "time out" afforded by a trading halt also serves a crucial, albeit sometimes understated, purpose: reducing information asymmetry. During periods of high volatility and rapid news flow, institutional investors with sophisticated information processing capabilities might react more swiftly than individual investors. A pause in trading allows for a broader assimilation of significant news or market movements across all participant types, potentially leading to more balanced and rational decision-making when trading resumes, thereby mitigating the risk of actions driven by incomplete or misunderstood information.

The Evolution of MWCBs

The genesis of stock market circuit breakers in the U.S. can be traced directly to the tumultuous events of "Black Monday"— October 19, 1987. On this day, the Dow Jones Industrial Average (DJIA) plummeted by an unprecedented 22.6% in a single trading session, sending shockwaves through global financial markets.[22] In the aftermath, the Presidential Task Force on Market Mechanisms, commonly known as the Brady Commission, was established to analyze the causes of the crash and recommend preventative measures. The Commission identified a lack of coordinated pauses across markets and the "illusion of liquidity" during the crisis as contributing factors, subsequently recommending the implementation of pre-determined trading halts, or circuit breakers.

The first iteration of circuit breakers was introduced by the New York Stock Exchange (NYSE) in 1988 and was based on absolute point declines in the DJIA. For instance, an initial 250-point drop in the DJIA would trigger a one-hour halt. This historical development underscores a pattern of reactive regulatory evolution, where significant market crises have directly spurred the creation and subsequent refinement of protective mechanisms. Just as Black Monday led to the first generation of market-wide circuit breakers, the "Flash Crash" of May 6, 2010, exposed vulnerabilities in addressing rapid, severe volatility in individual stocks. This event, where the DJIA dropped nearly 1,000 points in minutes only to recover quickly, highlighted the inadequacy of existing market-wide measures for such isolated incidents and became a key impetus for the development of the Limit Up-Limit Down (LULD) mechanism for individual securities.[23]

The evolution of circuit breakers also mirrors an ongoing adaptation to the increasing speed, complexity, and automation of financial markets. Program trading was cited as a contributing factor to the 1987 crash, while the Flash Crash was significantly influenced by algorithmic and high-frequency trading. Circuit breakers, in this context, represent an attempt to interject a human-paced "pause" into an increasingly machine-driven environment, aiming to prevent runaway feedback loops that can be amplified by automated trading strategies. Subsequent revisions, such as shifting from point-based to percentage-based triggers and adopting a broader market index (S&P 500), reflect a maturing understanding of market dynamics and a continuous effort to enhance the effectiveness of the critical market safeguards.

Governing Bodies and Rules:
The framework for MWCBs is established through rules approved by the U.S. Securities and Exchange Commission (SEC) and implemented by the national securities exchanges, such as the New York Stock Exchange (NYSE) and Nasdaq. These rules facilitate coordinated trading halts across all U.S. equity and options markets when severe market declines threaten to exhaust liquidity and destabilize markets. A significant evolution in these rules was the adoption of the S&P 500 Index as the single, unified reference for measuring market declines. This replaced the previous reliance on the Dow Jones Industrial Average (DJIA), reflecting a regulatory consensus

that the S&P 500, with its broader representation of the U.S. equity market, provides a more accurate and comprehensive benchmark for triggering such critical market interventions. This shift, along with the standardization of percentage-based thresholds and daily recalculations, points to a continuous effort by regulators to refine these mechanisms for greater transparency, representativeness, and responsiveness in maintaining market stability.

The MWCB System Structure

The MWCB system is structured around three levels of decline in the S&P 500 Index, measured against its closing price from the previous trading day:[24]

Level 1:
A 7% decline in the S&P 500. If the threshold is breached before 3:25 p.m. Eastern Time (ET), it triggers a 15-minute trading halt across all markets. If the breach occurs at or after 3:25 p.m. ET, trading generally continues without a halt, unless a Level 3 decline is subsequently triggered.

Level 2:
A 13% decline in the S&P 500 from the previous day's close. Similar to Level 1, if triggered before 3:25 p.m. ET, this results in a 15-minute, market-wide trading halt. If the breach occurs after 3:25 p.m. ET, trading generally continues barring a Level 3 trigger.

Level 3:
A 20% decline in the S&P 500 from the previous day's close. If

this level is reached at any time during the trading day, trading is halted for the remainder of that session across all markets.

The specific point values for these declines are recalculated daily by the exchanges based on the S&P 500's prior day closing level, ensuring the thresholds remain relevant to current market valuations. A Level 1 or Level 2 halt can only be triggered once per trading day. For instance, if a Level 1 halt occurs and trading resumes, another halt will not be triggered unless the market declines further to reach the Level 2 (13%) threshold. Exchanges like the NYSE have detailed protocols for managing order books during a halt and for conducting reopening auctions once trading is set to resume. While the technical function of MWCBs is to manage liquidity and allow market participants to process information during extreme volatility, they also serve a significant psychological purpose. By imposing a mandatory "cooling-off" period, these halts aim to interrupt panic selling and allow for a more orderly market readjustment. The infrequent activation of MWCBs, such as the instances during the market turmoil at the onset of the COVID-19 pandemic in March 2020, highlights their nature as an emergency intervention of last resort.

Limit Up-Limit Down (LULD) Rules

Distinct from market-wide halts, Limit Up-Limit Down (LULD) rules are designed to address sudden, extreme price movements in individual securities, including those that are constituents of the S&P 500.

The LULD rules apply broadly to National Market System (NMS) stocks and explicitly categorize all securities included in the S&P 500 Index as "Tier 1 NMS stocks". The primary goal of these single-security circuit breakers is to pause trading temporarily if an individual stock or exchange-traded product (ETP) moves outside a pre-defined price range within a short period, thereby preventing trades at clearly erroneous prices and moderating volatility.

The LULD mechanism establishes dynamic price bands for each Tier 1 security. These bands are typically set at 5% above and below the average price of the stock over the immediately preceding five-minute trading period. This 5% band applies during the majority of the trading session (9:30 a.m.–3:35 p.m. Eastern Time) for S&P 500 stocks with a previous day's closing price above $3.00. Near the market close (from 3:35 p.m.–4:00 p.m. Eastern Time), these price bands generally double to 10% for such securities. If a stock's price reaches one of these upper or lower bands and does not revert within 15 seconds, trading in that specific security is paused for five minutes.

The existence of LULD rules for S&P 500 constituents is significant because pronounced volatility in multiple large-cap components, each potentially triggering individual LULD halts, could collectively contribute to broader market instability. This phenomenon, sometimes referred to as a "contagion paradox", suggests that sharp declines in key index stocks can exert downward pressure on the overall S&P 500 Index level, potentially moving the market closer to the thresholds for a Market-Wide Circuit Breaker. Thus, while LULD halts are stock-specific, their aggregated impact in a stressed market scenario can have systemic implications.

The S&P 500 is not merely an abstract benchmark; it forms the foundation for a vast and complex ecosystem of tradable financial products, including ETPs (such as ETFs), options, and futures contracts. The behavior of these S&P 500-dependent products, particularly during periods of market stress, can itself trigger regulatory scrutiny and exchange-level actions.

Historical market stress events have revealed vulnerabilities in the trading of S&P 500-indexed ETPs. For example, during the market volatility on August 24, 2015, often referred to as an "ETF Stress Test", prominent ETPs designed to track the S&P 500, such as the SPDR S&P 500 ETF (SPY) and the iShares Core S&P 500 ETF (IVV), experienced significant deviations from the net asset value of the underlying index and from each other. This "unhinging" led to numerous trading halts in ETPs. On that day, a substantial majority (85%) of the 1,237 individual circuit breaker trading halts in U.S.-traded securities were in ETPs, many of which were based on large-cap indices like the S&P 500. Illustratively, the Powershares S&P 500 Low Volatility Portfolio (SPLV), an ETP designed to offer lower volatility, was itself halted 11 times, failing to meet its stated investment objective during the stress period.[25]

These events underscore a critical dependency: the orderly functioning of S&P 500-indexed ETPs relies heavily on overall market stability and liquidity. When these products misbehave or disconnect from their underlying index values, it can trigger exchange-level trading halts and prompt deeper regulatory investigation into their structure and market impact. Frequently, we only become aware of the risks after the fact. (Stick to the S&P 500 mutual fund from Vanguard, VFIAX.)

The regulatory framework for derivatives linked to the S&P 500 and its family of related indices is also influenced by the characteristics and established rules of the main index. Exchanges, such as CBOE Options, periodically propose rule changes to the SEC concerning products based on S&P

500-related indices. For instance, a proposal was made to amend position and exercise limits for options overlying the S&P 500 Equal Weight Index and the S&P 500 ESG Index. The rationale for such changes often references the existing regulatory treatment of options on the main S&P 500 Index (e.g. SPX options), which frequently have no position limits. The aim is to provide consistency for market participants employing hedging strategies across this family of related index products. This indicates that regulatory precedent set for the primary S&P 500 Index and its most liquid derivatives can shape the rules applied to newer or more specialized S&P 500-family indices, suggesting a harmonizing influence driven by the main index's established framework.

The complexity of this ecosystem means that regulators monitor not only the S&P 500 Index level itself but also the behavior of the myriad financial instruments tied to it. Issues within these dependent products can signal broader market stress or structural vulnerabilities, necessitating regulatory attention and potential intervention.

The S&P 500's Influence on the Federal Reserve

Beyond direct market intervention triggers, the S&P 500 Index and its associated data are deeply embedded in the statistical outputs, economic monitoring frameworks, and policy formulation processes of key U.S. government and regulatory agencies, most notably the Federal Reserve System and the Securities and Exchange Commission.

The Federal Reserve utilizes the S&P 500 in diverse ways, reflecting the index's importance as an indicator of financial market conditions and broader economic health.

<u>The FRED Database (Federal Reserve Economic Data):</u>
The Federal Reserve Bank of St. Louis plays a crucial role in public data dissemination through its FRED database. FRED includes daily S&P 500 Index values, explicitly recognizing the index as a key gauge of the U.S. large-cap equities market. By producing access to a decade of daily historical S&P 500 data, FRED facilitates economic research and analysis by academics, market participants, and the public, thereby cementing the S&P 500's status as an officially disseminated economic statistic.

<u>The Chicago Fed National Financial Conditions Index (NFCI):</u>
The Federal Reserve Bank of Chicago constructs and maintains the NFCI, a comprehensive weekly indicator of U.S. financial conditions. This index synthesizes information from 105 measures of financial activity, drawing from money markets, debt and equity markets, and the banking system. Data from equity markets, including the S&P 500 Total Return (SPTR) (which includes all dividends being reinvested), are incorporated into the NFCI. More broadly, equity market volatility, which is inherently linked to the behavior of the S&P 500, contributes to the "risk indicators" category within the NFCI. The NFCI is calibrated so that positive values suggest financial conditions are tighter than average, while negative values indicate looser conditions. While no specific S&P 500 level or change acts as a direct alert for the NFCI, its performance and volatility are integral components that contribute to the overall index value, which in turn informs the Federal Reserve's broader assessment of the prevailing financial environment.

<u>Financial Stability Oversight (Federal Reserve Board):</u>
The Board of Governors of the Federal Reserve System, in its

semi-annual Financial Stability Reports, explicitly uses metrics derived from the S&P 500 to assess "Asset Valuation Pressures". This is one of four key categories of vulnerabilities that the Fed monitors to gauge the resilience of the U.S. financial system. Specific S&P 500-related metrics prominently featured in these reports include:

- The aggregate forward price-to-earnings (P/E) ratio of S&P 500 firms. This ratio is compared against its historical median to identify periods of potentially stretched valuations. For instance, a P/E ratio reported as "well above its historical median" is a clear indicator of heightened valuation pressure.

- The equity risk premium (ERP), which represents the additional return investors expect for holding equities over risk-free assets. While not always directly quoted, it is often implicitly derived from S&P 500 earnings yields relative to government bond yields. A low or declining ERP can suggest that investors are demanding less compensation for bearing equity risk, potentially signaling increased risk appetite, overvaluation, or complacency in the market. These S&P 500-based valuation assessments are critical inputs into the Federal Reserve's overall judgment regarding potential risks to financial stability.

<u>Informing Policy (Countercyclical Capital Buffer—CCyB):</u>
The Federal Reserve's comprehensive assessment of financial vulnerabilities, which prominently includes the analysis of equity market valuations such as S&P 500 P/E ratios and the ERP, directly informs its decisions regarding the Countercyclical Capital Buffer (CCyB). The CCyB is a tool that allows the

Fed to require large banking organizations to hold additional capital during periods when systemic risks are judged to be accumulating. The buffer is intended to be raised when systemic vulnerabilities are "meaningfully above normal" and can be lowered or released when these risks abate or if the financial system comes under stress, thereby enabling banks to absorb losses and sustain lending.

Sustained periods of high S&P 500 valuations, rapid price appreciation, or increased volatility can contribute to an assessment of rising systemic risk, potentially leading the Fed to increase CCyB. Conversely, a sharp and sustained market downturn, signaled by the S&P 500, could contribute to a decision to reduce or release the buffer to support the financial system. While the CCyB is not mechanically triggered by a specific S&P 500 Index level, the index's performance is a significant input into the deliberative process for setting this important bank capital requirement. This demonstrates an indirect but powerful influence of S&P 500 market conditions on regulatory capital policy.

The Federal Reserve's extensive use of the S&P 500—as raw index levels, valuation ratios (P/E), total return figures, and volatility indicators—across diverse functions such as public data dissemination (FRED), composite financial condition index construction (NFCI), systemic risk assessment (Financial Stability Report), and bank capital policy calibration (CCyB) underscores a profound and multifaceted integration. This deep integration means the Fed's understanding of prevailing market conditions, financial stability, and potential systemic risks is significantly shaped by the behavior and characteristics of the S&P 500.

CHAPTER 7

CONTINUOUS IMPROVEMENT: 1957–PRESENT

Following its 1957 launch, the S&P 500 embarked on an evolutionary journey marked by several critical milestones. These developments enhanced its accessibility, utility, accuracy, and overall prominence, transforming it from a novel benchmark into an indispensable tool for global finance.

A pivotal moment in the S&P 500's history, and indeed in the history of modern investing, occurred on August 31, 1976. On this date, The Vanguard Group, under the leadership of John Bogle, introduced the first retail mutual fund designed to track the S&P 500 index. While its initial fundraising was modest—reportedly just $11 million[26]—the Vanguard 500 Index Fund grew exponentially over the decades, with assets under management reaching $1.48 trillion by the end of 2025.[27] This innovation was revolutionary because it democratized access to broad market returns. For the first time, ordinary individual investors could easily and at a low cost gain diversified exposure to a large segment of the U.S. stock market by simply investing in a single fund that aimed to replicate the performance of this key benchmark. This event was foundational to the subsequent explosion of passive investing.

The accessibility of the S&P 500 was further enhanced with the advent of exchange-traded funds (ETFs). On January 22, 1993, State Street Global Advisors (SSGA) launched the Standard & Poor's Depositary Receipts (SPDR) S&P 500 ETF, trading under the ticker symbol SPY. While preceded by the short-lived Index Participation Shares, SPY is widely recognized as the first successful ETF in the United States and has since become the world's largest and most actively traded ETF. ETFs like SPY combined the diversification benefits of index mutual funds with the intraday trading flexibility of individual stocks. This made investing in the S&P 500 even more convenient and liquid, significantly broadening its appeal to both individual and institutional investors. The immense trading volume in SPY also contributed to the price discovery process for the underlying S&P 500 constituent stocks.

The creation and subsequent widespread adoption of S&P 500 tracking index funds and ETFs established a powerful, self-reinforcing dynamic. As these passive investment vehicles attracted trillions of dollars in assets, the S&P 500's stature as the definitive U.S. equity benchmark grew commensurately. This increased prominence, in turn, spurred the development of even more financial products linked to the index. For a vast number of investors, "investing in the market" became synonymous with investing in an S&P 500 index fund or ETF. This widespread adoption fundamentally reshaped the investment management industry, fueling the meteoric rise of passive investing and cementing the S&P 500 as a central pillar of the global financial architecture.

The development of a sophisticated derivatives market based on the S&P 500 was another crucial set of milestones that significantly amplified its importance, particularly for institutional investors. On April 21, 1982, the Chicago Mercantile Exchange (CME) began trading futures contracts on the S&P 500 index. The introduction of S&P 500 futures provided institutional investors with a highly efficient and liquid tool for a variety of purposes, including hedging the risk of their equity portfolios, speculating on the future direction of the U.S. stock market, and executing arbitrage strategies between the futures and cash markets.

This was quickly followed by the introduction of options on the index. On July 1, 1983, the Chicago Board Options Exchange (CBOE, now Cboe Global Markets) launched trading in S&P 500 options (commonly known by the ticker SPX). These options, which are European-style (exercisable only at expiration) and cash-settled, offered market participants even more granular and flexible ways to manage risk, generate income, and express specific market views. The availability of both futures and options greatly deepened the S&P 500's integration into the operational fabric of financial markets.

The S&P 500 derivatives ecosystem was further broadened and democratized with the introduction of the S&P E-mini futures contract by the CME Group on September 9, 1997. The "E-mini" contract, being one-fifth the size of the standard S&P 500 futures contract, made futures trading on the index more accessible to a wider array of traders and smaller institutions due to its lower margin requirements and nominal value. This innovation significantly boosted trading volume and liquidity in the S&P 500-linked derivatives, further solidifying the index's central role.

The creation of this robust and highly liquid derivatives market was a key catalyst in the S&P 500's institutionalization as the primary U.S. equity benchmark. Large institutions require efficient mechanisms for managing portfolio risk, implementing tactical asset allocation shifts, and gaining broad market exposure without the transaction costs and complexities of trading hundreds of individual stocks. S&P 500 futures and options met these needs effectively. The deep liquidity and utility of these derivatives make the S&P 500 an indispensable tool for professional money managers, reinforcing its benchmark status. This demonstrated a powerful synergy: a liquid derivatives market enhances the utility of the underlying benchmark, leading to wider adoption and deeper integration into the financial market infrastructure.

Throughout its history, Standard & Poor's (and later SPDJI) has implemented several methodological and operational changes to enhance the S&P 500's accuracy, responsiveness, and relevance as a market benchmark. A significant operational improvement occurred in 1986 when the frequency of the index value updates dramatically increased. From that point forward, the S&P 500 value began to be calculated and disseminated every 15 seconds during the trading day, or 1,559 times daily, with price updates distributed by Reuters. Prior to this, the index had been updated only once every minute. This move to near real-time updates provided market participants with far more current information, making the index a more dynamic and responsive indicator of market changes, which was particularly crucial for the rapidly growing derivatives market and for active traders.

One of the most important methodological evolutions was the transition to float-adjusted market capitalization weightings in 2005.[28] Before this change, the index used total shares outstanding to calculate market capitalizations. The float-adjustment modified this by considering only those shares available for public trading, effectively excluding large, closely held blocks of stock (such as those held by governments, other corporations, insiders, or founding families) that are not readily available on the open market. S&P announced this change on March 1, 2004, and implemented it in two phases: a partial adjustment in March 2005 and full implementation in September 2005. This shift was a major enhancement, as it made the index *a more accurate reflection of the investable universe of stocks.* By weighting companies based on their public float, the index more closely mirrored the portfolio opportunities actually available to investors, thereby increasing its relevance and integrity as a benchmark for investment performance.

The adoption of the Global Industry Classification Standard (GICS) also marked a significant step in enhancing the analytical value of the S&P 500. GICS was jointly developed by MSCI and SPDJI in 1999. It provides a comprehensive, standardized, four-tiered hierarchical system for classifying companies into sectors, industry groups, industries, and sub-industries, and is applied consistently to companies globally. The S&P 500 utilizes GICS for its sector representation, which currently comprises 11 headline sectors (Real Estate having been added as the 11th sector in 2016, separating it from Financials). The use of GICS-standardized sector definitions across global markets, facilitating more precise sector-based investment strategies, performance attribution analysis, and cross-border comparisons.

The index is also subject to ongoing maintenance and rebalancing to reflect corporate actions such as mergers, acquisitions, spin-offs, and significant changes in market capitalization, and to ensure that its constituents continue to meet the prevailing eligibility criteria. While the S&P Composite 1500 indices (which include the S&P 500) do not have a fixed, scheduled reconstitution date for constituent changes (these are made on an "as-needed" basis), share counts are typically updated quarterly to reflect changes in shares outstanding.

These various methodological changes and ongoing refinements reflect a persistent effort by SPDJI to ensure the S&P 500 provides a "truer" and more accurate reflection of the investable U.S. large-cap equity market. As market structures evolved and the understanding of potential biases in index construction grew (such as the impact of large, non-tradable share blocks on simple market-cap weighting), the index methodology adapted. The 2005 transition to float adjustment, for example, was a direct response to the need to better represent the portion of company equity actually available to public investors. Similarly, the adoption of GICS improved analytical consistency and global comparability. This continuous process of refinement is vital for maintaining a benchmark's relevance, credibility, and trustworthiness in the eyes of its diverse users.

Market Volatility and Crisis Periods

The S&P 500's history is intertwined with periods of significant market volatility and crisis. These events have not only tested the resilience of the index and the broader market but have often served as catalysts for regulatory changes and shifts in market structure, ultimately influencing the index's role and prominence. Market crashes and recessions have invariably led to substantial declines in the S&P 500, underscoring its sensitivity to economic and financial shocks. However, a consistent theme throughout its history has been the eventual recovery from these downturns, although the duration and nature of these recoveries have varied significantly.

Black Monday (October 19, 1987) witnessed the S&P 500 plummet by approximately 20.47%, its largest single-day percentage drop in history.[29] As highlighted in Chapter 6, the Dow Jones Industrial Average fell an even steeper 22.6%. This dramatic crash was not an isolated event; it was preceded by a significant market decline in the preceding week, during which the S&P 500 had already lost over 9–10% of its value.[30] The causes of Black Monday are generally attributed to a confluence of factors, including the relatively new phenomenon of computerized program trading (particularly portfolio insurance strategies), widespread investor panic, a preceding strong bull market that may have led to overvaluation, and macroeconomic concerns such as the U.S. dollar's decline and the trade deficit. The crash triggered a global stock market downturn and exposed critical weaknesses in existing market trading systems. A significant outcome was the subsequent introduction of market-wide "circuit breakers"—mechanisms designed to temporarily halt trading during periods of extreme market decline, now explicitly tied to percentage drops in the S&P 500 Index itself. This event, while a severe test of market stability, paradoxically helped to cement the S&P 500's importance by integrating it into the very fabric of market safety protocols.

The late 1990s were characterized by a speculative frenzy in internet and technology-related stocks, leading to a massive run-up in valuations. The S&P 500 nearly doubled in value during this boom period, only to suffer a decline of almost 45% when the bubble burst between 2000 and 2002. The tech-heavy Nasdaq 100 experienced an even more dramatic plunge of over 80%.[31] The S&P 500 reached a record high in March 2000 that it would not surpass again until 2007. During the peak of the bubble, the Information Technology sector's weight in the S&P 500 had swelled to 33% (June 2000), and the concentration of the top 10 stocks in the index approached 30%.[32] The bursting of the bubble demonstrated the S&P 500's capacity to reflect, and be vulnerable to, speculative excesses and significant sectoral shifts. It ushered in what some termed a "lost decade" (roughly 2000–2009) for broad market returns, during which the S&P 500's price level fell from 1320.28 on 12/29/2000 to 903.25 on 12/31/2008.[33]

The Global Financial Crisis (GFC) (2007–2009), originating in the U.S. subprime mortgage market, escalated into a global financial meltdown, leading to the failure or near-failure of major financial institutions (such as the bankruptcy of Lehman Brothers on September 15, 2008) and triggering a severe global recession. The S&P 500 was profoundly affected, falling 56.8% from its peak in October 2007 to its trough in March 2009. In the calendar year 2008 alone, the index recorded a decrease of 38.5%.[34] The GFC prompted unprecedented government bailouts, aggressive monetary policy interventions by central banks (including deep interest rate cuts and quantitative easing programs), and sweeping financial regulatory reforms, most notably the Dodd-Frank Wall Street Reform and Consumer Protection Act in the U.S. The S&P 500 served as a critical barometer for the depth of this systemic crisis and the subsequent, often arduous, recovery. It took until

March 2013 for the index to fully recoup its losses from the GFC.

The sudden onset of the global COVID-19 pandemic in early 2020 led to widespread economic shutdowns and immense uncertainty. Equity markets reacted violently, with the S&P 500 plummeting approximately 34% in just over a month, from February 19, 2020, to March 23, 2020.[35] The velocity of the decline triggered market circuit breakers on multiple occasions. In response, governments and central banks globally unleashed unprecedented levels of fiscal and monetary stimulus, which fueled an extraordinarily rapid market recovery. The S&P 500 reached new all-time highs by August 2020. The pandemic also highlighted stark divergences in sectoral performance, with technology and online retail companies proving resilient or even thriving, while sectors like travel, hospitality, and traditional retail faced severe challenges. The S&P 500's performance was a key focal point for assessing economic and market health during this unparalleled global crisis.

In more recent years, the S&P 500 has demonstrated sensitivity to various macroeconomic and geopolitical factors, including U.S.-China trade tensions and the implementation of tariffs. Such events have often caused significant short-term volatility in the index. For instance, periods of heightened tariff rhetoric and implementation have reportedly led to notable declines in liquidity for S&P 500 E-mini futures. These episodes reinforce the S&P 500's role as an indicator of broad market sentiment in response to global economic policy shifts and geopolitical uncertainties.

The history of the S&P 500's navigation through these crises reveals a pattern: while market downturns pose immediate threats to investor capital and confidence, they often serve as powerful catalysts for regulatory evolution and improvements in market structure. Events like Black Monday directly led to the implementation of circuit breakers, which are based on S&P 500 percentage declines, thereby embedding the index into the market's safety mechanisms. Similarly, the Global Financial Crisis spurred comprehensive reforms like the Dodd-Frank Act, aimed at bolstering financial stability, with the S&P 500 acting as a primary gauge of market health throughout the reform process and its aftermath. The S&P 500's prominence is not solely a function of its design but also a consequence of its deep integration into the regulatory and operational fabric of the U.S. financial system. The index's consistent ability to recover from these shocks has also, over the long term, bolstered investor confidence in the U.S. equity market it represents.

S&P 500 Governance Structure

The credibility and widespread acceptance of the S&P 500 are underpinned by a formal governance structure and its interaction with regulatory bodies and international standards. The primary stewardship of the S&P 500 rests with the S&P U.S. Index Committee (often referred to simply as the Index Committee). This body is responsible for maintaining the S&P U.S. Indices, which includes making critical decisions regarding constituent selection (additions and deletions), overseeing and approving methodology changes, and determining the appropriate treatment of various corporate actions (such as mergers, spin-offs, stock splits, and special dividends) that affect index constituents. The overarching goal of the committee is to ensure that the index remains a representative and reliable measure of the U.S. equity market, particularly the large-cap segment, and reflects leading companies in leading industries.

The Index Committee is composed of full-time professional members of SPDJI' staff. Crucially, SPDJI states that its voting members on the Index Committees are senior individuals who have no commercial responsibilities, a measure intended to mitigate potential conflicts of interest. The committee typically meets on a monthly basis to review pending corporate actions, analyze market statistics comparing the composition of indices to the broader market, evaluate companies that are candidates for addition to an index, and discuss any significant market events that may warrant attention. While decisions are guided by established, publicly available methodologies, the committee may exercise expert judgment and discretion in exceptional circumstances not explicitly addressed by the rules, or to avoid outcomes like unnecessary constituent turnover or potential market disruption.

SPDJI emphasizes its commitment to robust and transparent benchmarks. Its governance policies include provisions for public consultations before implementing material methodology changes. These consultations generally provide a minimum one-month period for market participants to provide feedback. Furthermore, index methodologies are subject to review at least annually to ensure they continue to meet their stated objectives and remain effective. Announcements regarding changes to the index, such as constituent additions or deletions, are disseminated through the S&P Global website and major news services, typically after market close to allow for orderly adjustment by market participants. The evolution of this governance framework towards more formalized procedures and public consultation reflects broader trends in the industry toward greater accountability and transparency in benchmark administration.

The S&P 500 operates within a landscape shaped by regulatory requirements and international best practices. In the United States, the Securities and Exchange Commission (SEC) has rules that indirectly bolster the prominence of benchmarks like the S&P 500. For instance, the SEC requires registered investment companies (such as mutual funds and ETFs) to compare their historical performance against that of an appropriate "broad-based securities market index" in prospectuses and other regulatory filings. The S&P 500 is a very common choice for this purpose. Additionally, the SEC mandates that companies included in the S&P 500 must disclose their own stock performance relative to the Index in their annual 10-K filings. These regulatory requirements effectively endorse the use of established benchmarks and contribute to their institutionalization.

On an international level, the Principles of Financial Benchmarks developed by the International Organization of Securities Commissions (IOSCO) have become a global standard for benchmark administration. These principles, formulated in the wake of benchmark manipulation scandals such as LIBOR, address key areas including governance, the quality and integrity of the benchmark methodology, the quality of data inputs, and transparency and accountability procedures. SPDJI has publicly stated its support for and adherence to the IOSCO Principles. SPDJI has also engaged independent third-party firms, such as Ernst & Young, to conduct annual reviews of its control framework's alignment with the IOSCO Principles, and publishes these assurance reports. This adherence to international standards is crucial for maintaining the global credibility and integrity of SPDJI's benchmarks, including the

S&P 500, signaling a commitment to robust governance and transparent operational practices.

The governance of a benchmark as influential as the S&P 500 inherently involves a complex balancing act. It requires adherence to transparent, rules-based methodologies while simultaneously allowing for a degree of expert discretion to navigate the complexities of real-world market events and maintain the index's representativeness and investability. Criticisms regarding market concentration, the "active" component of committee decisions, or the nuances of transparency often put pressure on benchmark administrators like SPDJI. This external scrutiny, combined with evolving industry best practices and heightened regulatory expectations (such as the IOSCO Principles), drives continuous refinements to governance structures, methodological documentation, and public communication strategies. The S&P 500's ability to maintain its widespread credibility and trust hinges on its success in navigating this intricate interplay of rules, judgment, and the diverse expectations of its global stakeholders. This process is not static but reflects the broader financial industry's ongoing movement towards greater transparency, accountability, and robustness in benchmark administration, particularly in the aftermath of events that have shaken confidence in other key financial benchmarks.

S&P 500 Futures and Options

S&P 500 futures and options are among the most actively traded and liquid derivative contracts globally. This high liquidity is paramount, as it allows market participants to execute large trades quickly and with minimal price impact, providing efficient tools for managing exposure to the U.S. equity market. Institutional investors, who manage vast pools of capital, widely use S&P 500 derivatives to hedge their portfolio risk against broad market downturns. The ability to effectively and cost-efficiently hedge systemic market risk using S&P 500 derivatives is a critical function that makes the index indispensable for large asset managers, pension funds, and insurance companies.

Beyond hedging, these derivatives also facilitate speculation on market direction and the implementation of complex trading strategies. Furthermore, trading activity in the S&P 500 futures and options markets plays a significant role in the price discovery process for the broader U.S. equity market. Derivatives markets often react very quickly to new information or shifts in sentiment, and these price signals are closely watched by participants in the cash equity market, influencing trading decisions there. The E-mini S&P 500 futures contract, introduced in 1997, further enhanced this ecosystem by broadening access to futures trading and thereby increasing overall trading volumes and liquidity.

The needs of sophisticated institutional investors often dictate which benchmarks become industry standards. The S&P 500's success in fostering a deep, liquid, and highly functional derivatives market around it was a key differentiator that contributed significantly to its ascendancy over other indices, like the DJIA, for institutional benchmarking and risk management purposes. The DJIA, while iconic, historically lacked a comparable derivatives complex in terms of the depth, breadth, and intensity of use by institutions for these core portfolio management functions. Academic research also points to the impact of derivatives on market microstructure and liquidity, further underscoring their importance.[36] This robust ecosystem of S&P 500-linked products—spanning cash-tracking funds and ETFs to highly liquid derivatives—created a powerful network effect. As more investors, financial products, and trading activities centered on the S&P 500, its value and utility to all other market participants increased, making it progressively more entrenched as the standard.

The S&P 500 Quality Management Ecosystem

S&P Global's long-term strategy has been to control and continuously refine the entire intellectual supply chain of index construction. This approach rejects the notion of an index as a static product and instead treats it as a dynamic service that must constantly adapt and improve to maintain its quality and relevance. This philosophy manifests itself as a powerful web of interconnected activities that form a holistic, self-reinforcing ecosystem for quality management.

This ecosystem consists of three core pillars:

Input Quality & Control:
The strategic creation and management of foundational data and classification systems. This includes the development of Compustat to standardize the raw material of financial data and the co-creation of the Global Industry Classification Standard (GICS) to bring logical order to the market universe. These initiatives represent a foundational commitment to ensuring that all subsequent decisions are based on the highest-quality inputs.

Process Improvement:
The iterative evolution of the S&P 500's core methodology. This involves tracing the incremental but transformative changes—

such as the shift to float-adjusted market capitalization and the implementation of a strict profitability criterion—that have fundamentally enhanced the index's integrity and investability.

<u>Dynamic Renewal:</u>
The constant re-evaluation and turnover of the constituent companies, managed by the S&P Dow Jones Index Committee. This pillar focuses on the active stewardship that ensures the index remains a portfolio of leading companies, perpetually reflecting the "creative destruction" and innovation inherent in the U.S. economy.

The business of creating a market-cap-weighted index can, at its surface, appear to be a commodity. Many providers possess the technical capability to calculate a weighted average of stock prices. However, there is a deeper strategic layer that differentiates S&P Global's approach. The relentless focus on process control, input quality, standardization, and incremental improvement constitutes a formidable, non-obvious competitive moat. While competitors may emphasize different virtues, such as the rigid transparency of a purely rules-based system, S&P's strategy is a profound investment in the quality of the process itself. This cultural and operational commitment, viewing the index not as a static product but as a dynamic, continuously improving service, is the fundamental source of the "quality" that defines the S&P 500. It transforms the index from a simple calculation into a sophisticated, managed intellectual product.

A core tenet of any quality management philosophy is that the quality of the final product is dependent on the quality of its raw materials. In the context of index construction, the primary inputs are not physical but intellectual: financial data and a logical system for classification. S&P Global's history demonstrates a profound understanding of this principle. Rather than passively accepting the variable quality of publicly available information, the company took decisive steps to control and improve its most critical inputs. This proactive strategy of vertically integrating the intellectual supply chain, executed through the creation of Compustat and the co-development of the Global Industry Classification Standard (GICS), is continuous improvement in action.

Compustat

Prior to the mid-20th century, the world of financial analysis was characterized by a chaotic lack of standardization. Every public company filed financial reports, but the presentation of this information varied wildly. Important data points could be found in tables, narrative descriptions, or buried deep within footnotes, making rigorous "apples-to-apples" comparisons between companies a Herculean task for analysts. This was a fundamental quality control problem at the very start of the index construction process, introducing noise, inefficiency, and the potential for error.

S&P's response to this challenge was a revolutionary act of process control. The launch of the Compustat database in 1962 was far more than the creation of a data repository; it was the establishment of a standardization engine. Compustat's mission was to ingest the messy, non-uniform world of corporate financial reporting and output clean, consistent, and comparable data. This is achieved through a meticulous process where S&P analysts review every report, extract relevant numbers from their disparate locations, and recast them into a uniform, analytically coherent format.

The specific ways Compustat enhances input quality are numerous and profound:

Standardize Core Earnings:

GAAP (Generally Accepted Accounting Principles) allows for wide variations in how companies report earnings. To address this, Compustat developed the concept of "core earnings" , a uniform methodology for calculating a company's operating profitability. This standardized metric is designed to focus on after-tax earnings generated from a company's principal business activities. It ensures that typical operational costs, such as employee stock options and pension expenses, are fully attributed, while excluding significant non-operating items like gains or losses from asset sales. This provides a much clearer and more comparable view of a firm's sustainable profitability, a critical input for the Index Committee's financial viability assessment.

Standardize Peer Group Comparisons:

The true power of standardized data is its ability to enable meaningful comparisons. By putting every company's financials into the same format, Compustat allows for the calculation of reliable industry and sector norms for crucial performance ratios like return on assets, price-to-cash flow, and net margin. It then ranks each company against its peers, as determined by GICS for large-cap companies, allowing analysts and the Index Committee to objectively gauge management effectiveness and competitive positioning.

Data Integrity and Accuracy:

The process is underpinned by a dual system of human and automated quality control. Analysts review reports for adherence to Compustat's rigorous presentation formats, and automated systems perform a wide array of internal checks to ensure data consistency and integrity. This relentless focus on quality ensures that the foundational data used to evaluate companies for the S&P 500 is as accurate and reliable as possible.

By creating Compustat, S&P was not merely collecting data; it was manufacturing a higher grade of raw material for its own core business. This strategic decision gave it an unparalleled advantage in the quality and consistency of its inputs, improving the process at its most fundamental level.

The Global Industry Classification Standard (GICS)

While Compustat standardized the financial data of individual companies, a second, equally critical problem remained: the lack of a coherent system for organizing the companies themselves. Before 1999, the financial world relied on a patchwork of industry classification systems. These systems were often designed for tracking national economic output (GDP), not for investment analysis. They were frequently specific to a single geographic region, overrepresented industries with few publicly traded companies (like agriculture), and failed to reflect the modern, globalized economy.

The solution came in 1999, when S&P, in a landmark partnership with MSCI, developed and launched the Global Industry Classification Standard (GICS). The goal was to create a single, comprehensive, and transparent global standard designed specifically for the needs of the investment community. GICS provided a logical, hierarchical framework that brought order to the entire market universe, serving as a critical tool for both the Index Committee and the broader financial world.

The design of GICS provided an intellectual framework for consistent and standardized classification:

Hierarchical Structure:

GICS employs a four-tiered structure that cascades from broad to specific: 11 Sectors, 25 Industry Groups, 74 Industries, and 163 Sub-Industries (as of early 2026)[37]. This elegant hierarchy allows users, including the S&P Index Committee, to analyze the market at any desired level of granularity. It provides the flexibility to ensure broad sector balance in the index while also allowing for deep, nuanced analysis at the sub-industry level.

Investment-Focused Methodology:

Unlike its predecessors, GICS classifies companies based on their principal business activity, using revenues as a key determinant but also considering earnings and market perception. This approach is fundamentally investor-centric, grouping companies based on how they compete and how their stocks are likely to behave in similar economic conditions, which is far more relevant for portfolio construction than older, production-oriented models.

Continuous Evolution:

Perhaps the most compelling feature of GICS is that the standard itself is subject to continuous improvement. MSCI and S&P conduct annual reviews to ensure the GICS structure remains representative of the evolving global economy. This has led to major, well-communicated updates that reflect significant economic shifts. For example, the separation of Real Estate from the Financials sector and the creation of the Communication Services sector (carved out from Technology and Consumer Discretionary) demonstrate that the tool used to improve the S&P 500 is itself being perpetually refined.

The development and control of Compustat and GICS represent a deliberate and powerful strategy of vertically integrating the intellectual supply chain of index construction. S&P Global identified that the most significant risks to the quality of its flagship product were inconsistent data and illogical classification. Instead of mitigating these risks by relying on third-party sources, it chose to eliminate them by creating and controlling its own proprietary, best-in-class systems. This created a closed-loop ecosystem where S&P manages the entire process, from the initial collection and standardization of raw corporate filings to the final classification and selection of companies for the index. This control over the foundational inputs is a massive, often-overlooked competitive advantage that ensures all "downstream" decisions made by the Index Committee are built upon the most solid and consistent "upstream" foundation possible.

The Index Methodology

If controlling the quality of inputs is the foundation of S&P Global's approach, then the continuous, incremental improvement of the index's core construction methodology by the Index Committee is the architectural framework built upon it. An index methodology is the set of rules—the blueprint—that defines how constituents are selected, weighted, and maintained. A static blueprint in a dynamic market quickly becomes obsolete. The S&P 500 index's "recipe" has been subject to a series of deliberate, data-driven refinements designed to enhance its quality, representativeness, and investability.

For much of its early history, the S&P 500, like other indices of its era, was weighted by full market capitalization. This method calculates a company's weight by multiplying its share price by its total number of outstanding shares. The critical flaw in this approach was that it included all shares, even those locked up and unavailable for public trading. These "inactive" shares, often held by company insiders, founding families, governments, or other corporations, distorted the true picture of the market. An index weighted this way did not accurately represent the opportunity set actually available to public investors, making it a less precise and less replicable benchmark for the burgeoning world of index funds and ETFs.

The Index Committee transitioned the S&P 500 calculation to a free-float-adjusted methodology to address this issue. This significant but incremental change altered the calculation to consider only the "free-floating" shares—those readily available for trading on the open market. The Investable Weight Factor (IWF) was introduced to systematically exclude locked-in shares from the market capitalization calculation.

The float-adjusted index provided a more accurate reflection of market movements and the stocks actively available for investment. It reduced the influence of companies with large, closely held blocks of stock, which could otherwise have an outsized weight relative to their actual impact on the public market. This refinement made the S&P 500 a more investable and replicable benchmark—a direct improvement in its value as defined by its primary customers: portfolio managers and investors seeking to track its performance.

A purely size-based index, even one that is float-adjusted, risks including companies that are large but financially precarious. A large market capitalization can sometimes reflect investor hype or momentum rather than underlying business strength, potentially introducing undue volatility and risk into the benchmark. Recognizing this potential weakness, the S&P Index Committee implemented a crucial methodological enhancement: a strict financial viability criterion.

To be eligible for inclusion in the S&P 500, a company must demonstrate sustained profitability. Specifically, the sum of its most recent four consecutive quarters' as-reported GAAP earnings must be positive, and its most recent quarter's earnings must also be positive. This rule acts as a powerful, non-negotiable quality filter.

The result is that the S&P 500 is not merely a list of the 500 largest U.S. companies. It is a curated portfolio of the largest, leading, and profitable companies in the nation's leading industries. This fundamentally alters the character of the index and serves as a key point of differentiation from many of its competitors. For instance, the purely rules-based Russell 1000 index lacks a comparable profitability hurdle, meaning it can and does include large, unprofitable companies, which can affect its risk and return profile. The S&P 500's profitability rule is a deliberate choice to prioritize financial health and stability over pure size, embedding a layer of quality directly into the index's DNA.

This profitability mandate can be understood as a de facto "quality factor" screen, predating the widespread popularity of explicit factor investing strategies. Modern quantitative finance often targets factors like "Quality," which includes metrics such as high profitability, stable earnings, and strong balance sheets. The S&P 500's financial viability rule has effectively been applying such a screen for decades. This reframes the index not as a generic "vanilla" market-cap benchmark, but as a more sophisticated "market-cap plus quality" portfolio. This built-in quality tilt helps to explain the index's historical resilience and long-term performance.

The "metabolism" of the index itself is its selection mechanism: the constant shedding of companies that no longer meet its high standards and the absorption of new leaders that do. It is a fundamental point of distinction between the S&P 500 and many of its peers. The constituent companies of the S&P 500 are ultimately selected by the Index Committee, a group of full-time, professional S&P staff who convene monthly to review candidates, pending corporate actions, and overall market representation.

While the committee operates within the strict quantitative guidelines for size, liquidity, and profitability, it retains a crucial layer of discretion. This human judgment allows for a more nuanced application of the rules. The committee can consider qualitative factors, such as a company's leadership position within its industry and the need to maintain sector balance across the index, that a rigid formula might miss.

This discretionary power has fueled a long-standing academic debate about whether an index managed by a committee can truly be considered "passive". Critics argue that the committee's choices introduce an active management component. It is not active management in the traditional sense of trying to "beat the market". Rather, it is a form of active stewardship or "intelligent indexing" aimed at maintaining the quality and representativeness of the benchmark. This stewardship is a form of continuous oversight and quality control.

This human oversight acts as a critical buffer against the potential for algorithmic fragility. Purely rules-based systems, while transparent, can be gamed or can produce unintended and illogical outcomes when faced with novel or complex corporate events. The Index Committee serves as a human-in-the-loop safeguard. Their discretion allows them to interpret the spirit of the rules, not just the letter. For example, the committee has the discretion to keep a stock in the index if it is temporarily halted from trading, or to make a final determination on a company's domicile when quantitative factors are ambiguous. This provides a layer of robustness and common-sense oversight that prevents the index from being slavishly driven by a formula that might not capture the full economic context. This consistent application of human judgment, within a disciplined framework of continuous improvement, becomes a defining feature of the index's quality, not a bug.

The S&P 500's approach is more fluid and continuous. Changes are typically made on an "as-needed" basis. A vacancy in the index is usually created when a constituent company is removed because of a merger, acquisition, delisting, bankruptcy, or a substantial and sustained decline that causes it to violate the inclusion criteria. Only then does the Index Committee select a replacement from its list of eligible candidates that best fits the index's needs at that time.

This process of constant, incremental turnover ensures that the S&P 500 perpetually reflects the dynamic nature of the U.S. economy. It systematically purges companies that have faltered and embraces emerging leaders that have risen to meet its stringent criteria. This process mirrors the economic principle of "creative destruction", allowing the index to evolve organically with the market. Over the decades, this has meant a shift away from a heavy concentration in traditional industrial and energy companies toward the technology and healthcare giants that define the modern economy. Without this metabolic process of renewal, the S&P 500 would quickly become a relic, a museum of past economic glories rather than a vibrant reflection of its present and future. This continuous re-evaluation and replacement is the ultimate expression of the committee's judgment.

CHAPTER 8

S&P 500 INVESTMENT ATTRIBUTES: THE PARETO PRINCIPLE, CONCENTRATION AND FAT TAILS

Don't look for the needle, just buy the haystack.

—Jack Bogle

The Pareto Principle, also known as the 80/20 rule, is an empirical observation suggesting that for many events, roughly 80% of the effects come from 20% of the causes. This principle highlights an inherently unequal relationship between inputs and outputs across a wide array of phenomena. The enduring power of the Pareto Principle lies not in the precision of its numerical ratio but in its fundamental assertion of non-linearity and unequal distribution as inherent characteristics of complex systems.

Financial markets, being intricate adaptive systems with

numerous interacting agents and feedback loops, are prime candidates for exhibiting such imbalances. Therefore, we should anticipate these skewed distributions in market phenomena rather than viewing them as anomalies. Said another way, we should expect most of the results to be driven by a handful of companies. The principle's applicability across varied and unrelated domains suggests that it captures a fundamental property of many systems where resources, efforts, or causes are not uniformly effective or impactful. This makes it a particularly useful lens for analyzing the dynamics of equity markets.

When applied to the realm of finance and investments, the Pareto Principle suggests that a disproportionately large share of portfolio gains will originate from a relatively small percentage of the underlying investments. For example, it is often said that 80% of a portfolio's returns could be generated by just 20% of its holdings. This concept is intrinsically linked to the statistical property of skewness observed in investment return distributions. Equity returns, in particular, are characterized by positive skewness, meaning that the distribution is not symmetrical like a bell curve but has a long tail on the right side. This "fat tail" signifies that while most returns may cluster around a modest positive future, there are a few instances of exceptionally large positive outcomes. These outliers pull the arithmetic mean (average) return significantly above the median (middle) return, indicating that the "typical" experience is different from the average. A few big winners will pull up the average. A great example is just before the S&P 500 was launched. S&P had two indices, the S&P 90 that was calculated daily and the S&P 480 that was calculated weekly. The two index values were nearly identical in the 50s, indicating the significant impact that the largest 90 companies had on the larger index. This is true today when you compare the returns of the S&P 500 with the total U.S. stock market that has almost 4,000 companies in it. The S & P 500 drives the returns for the entire market.

The most compelling evidence for this Pareto-like concentration in equity market returns comes from academic research, notably the work of Professor Hendrik Bessembinder. His extensive studies of long-term stock performance in the U.S. market have demonstrated that a remarkably small fraction of publicly traded companies accounts for the vast majority of net wealth creation over extended periods. For instance, one of Bessembinder's analyses covering the period from 1926 to 2022 found that just 3.4% of all listed stocks generated 100% of the $55 trillion in aggregate net wealth created by the entire U.S. stock market. The remaining 96.6% of stocks, in aggregate, produced returns that merely matched those of one-month Treasury bills.[38]

These findings imply that the "average" stock does not perform nearly as well as commonly perceived market index returns might suggest. In fact, most individual stocks underperform risk-free assets over their lifetimes, and the median lifetime compound return for an individual stock can even be negative. This stark difference between the mean and median outcomes for individual stocks powerfully illustrates a Pareto-like distribution in long-term stock performance, where a "vital few" generate most of the market's overall gains. The extreme positive skewness highlighted by this research underscores that the traditional focus on "average" market returns can be misleading when trying to understand the typical individual stock's journey. The market's overall success is overwhelmingly built upon the extraordinary performance of a select few winners. This reality highlights the inherent difficulty of active stock picking—the probability of randomly selecting one of these few "vital" stocks is low—and provides a strong empirical basis for the benefits of broad diversification, which increases an investor's chances of capturing these outsized winners.

The observation that a small number of stocks drive the majority of market gains is also consistent with the concept of power-law distributions in stock performance. In a power-law distribution, the tail representing extreme outperformers declines much more slowly than it would in a normal (Gaussian) distribution. This means that exceptionally large outcomes, while rare, are far more probable and impactful than traditional financial models based on normal distributions might predict. This power-law nature of stock returns further implies that these extreme positive "black swan" events, though infrequent for any single stock, are not only possible but are integral to the market's aggregate long-term performance. Financial models that fail to account for these fat-tailed distributions may underestimate the potential upside driven by these outliers, or conversely, misjudge the risk of constructing a portfolio that inadvertently misses these few crucial contributors.

The success of market capitalization-weighted indices, such as the S&P 500, is intrinsically linked to this Pareto-like distribution of returns. By design, these indices allocate capital based on the current market value of their constituent companies. As certain companies achieve superior performance and their market capitalization grows, their weighting within the index automatically increases. This mechanism ensures that the index "lets its winners ride" thereby capturing the significant contributions of these vital few stocks that drive overall market wealth. This inherent feature is a key reason for the long-term success of market-cap-weighted passive investment vehicles.

The "concentration risk" frequently discussed is how the index generates exceptional returns. The only way to lessen the concentration would be to sell the stocks that increase, similar to what happens in an equal-weight index, and then buy the stocks that are performing poorly. You would need to "sell the winners and buy the losers".

The Index's Concentration Over Time

The market-capitalization-weighted nature of the S&P 500 has historically led to varying degrees of concentration, where a relatively small number of top holdings account for a significant portion of the index's total market value. The weight of the top 10 companies in the S&P 500 has seen considerable fluctuation over the decades. For instance:

- In 1990, the top 10 stocks constituted approximately 20% of the index's market capitalization.[39]
- During the peak of the dot-com bubble around the year 2000, this concentration rose, with the top 10 companies representing between 26% and just under 30% of the index.[40]
- The "Magnificent Seven" stocks alone (a subset of the top 10) held an approximate 40% weighting in the index at the end of 2025.[41]

The following table highlights the top 10's market capitalization over time.

Year	Top 10	Top 5 company names
1972 (Nifty Fifty)	Estimated 25–30% [42]	IBM, Eastman Kodak, Procter & Gamble, Sears, GE
1980	22% [43]	IBM, AT&T, Exxon, GE, Schlumberger
1990	20% [44]	Exxon, GE, IBM, Philip Morris, Merck
2000 (Dot-com peak)	26–30% [45]	Microsoft, GE, Cisco, Intel, ExxonMobil
2009 (GFC low)	19% [46]	ExxonMobil, Microsoft, Procter & Gamble, Johnson & Johnson, AT&T
2020	30–34% [47]	Apple, Microsoft, Amazon, Alphabet (Google), Facebook (Meta)
2025	34–40% [48]	Microsoft, Apple, Nvidia, Amazon, Alphabet (Google)

Table 8-1

The market-capitalization weightings of the S&P 500 directly translate into a concentration of returns, whereby the performance of the largest constituents disproportionately impacts the overall index return. When these top stocks experience significant price movements, the entire index tends to follow suit. This phenomenon is a direct manifestation of the Pareto Principle: a vital few stocks often drive the S&P 500's performance. Academic work by Bessembinder and others, showing that a small number of stocks dramatically outperform and contribute most to long-run portfolio returns, finds its practical expression in the behavior of cap-weighted indices.

Recent examples are particularly stark. In 2024, a single company, Nvidia, was reported to have accounted for almost a quarter (23%) of the S&P 500's growth in market capitalization.[49] The "Magnificent Seven" group of technology-related stocks has been credited with driving nearly all of the stock market's gains in the 2023–2024 period; without their contribution, the S&P 500 would have reportedly registered minimal gains.[50] This pattern is not new; different market leaders have similarly influenced index returns in past eras, such as the "Nifty Fifty" in the 1970s and the leading technology stocks during the late 1990s.

The dynamic composition of the S&P 500—the ongoing process of adding and removing companies—means that long-term studies of "S&P 500" returns are not tracking a fixed basket of securities. The index itself evolves to capture the prevailing "vital few". This adaptive quality is a form of embedded momentum and a significant reason for its long-term success. However, it also complicates direct historical comparisons of constituent contributions if survivorship bias is not carefully considered. The index's methodology, by design, tends to replace lagging companies with rising stars, thereby inherently seeking to reflect the successful 20% (or an even smaller fraction) over time. This means the "causes"—the specific stocks driving the concentrated outcomes—are not static but change with market evolution.

In the late 1960s and early 1970s, a group of approximately 50 large-cap stocks, perceived as stable, high-growth companies, became market darlings. These "Nifty Fifty" stocks, including names like IBM, Coca-Cola, McDonald's, Polaroid, and Xerox, were considered "one-decision" stocks; buy and hold indefinitely. This investor sentiment led to significant market concentration and pushed the valuations of these companies to extreme levels. The Nifty Fifty, on average, traded at price-to-earnings (P/E) ratios more than double that of the broader S&P 500 average. For example, Polaroid reportedly traded at a P/E of 91 times earnings at its peak, while the group overall commanded P/Es around 42x when the S&P 500 was at 19x.[51] However, this era of high concentration and lofty valuations was followed by a period of significant underperformance for many of these favored stocks during the bear market of 1973–1974 and beyond. Studies indicate that the top half of the Nifty Fifty cohort materially underperformed the broader S&P 500 over the subsequent years.[52]

The late 1990s saw another wave of market concentration, this time centered around technology, media, and telecommunication (TMT) stocks fueled by the internet boom. Valuations for companies in these sectors, many with limited earnings or unproven business models, reached unprecedented levels. As highlighted in the table earlier in this chapter, at the dot-com peak in 2000, the top 10 companies in the S&P 500 accounted for approximately 26–30% of the index's market capitalization. Similar to the aftermath of the Nifty Fifty era, the bursting of the dot-com bubble led to a sharp decline and prolonged underperformance for many of the leading, highly valued technology stocks. For example, from the peak in March 2000 through October 2002, the technology-heavy Nasdaq Composite Index fell nearly 80%[53], and the Russell 1000 Growth Index declined over 57% from its 2000 peak through 2008.[54]

While there are parallels between the dot-com era and current market concentration, there are also notable differences. Today's largest technology companies, often referred to as the "Magnificent Seven", generally possess much stronger fundamentals, including substantial earnings, robust profitability, and higher returns on equity compared to many of the speculative leaders of the dot-com era. Their current P/E is around 27, compared to a P/E of 50 for market leaders during the dot-com peak.

In recent years, a new group of mega-cap technology-oriented stocks—Apple, Microsoft, Alphabet (Google), Amazon, Nvidia, Meta (Facebook), and Tesla, collectively dubbed the "Magnificent Seven"—has driven a significant portion of the S&P 500's returns and market capitalization concentration. These seven stocks began 2023 constituting about 20% of the S&P 500, a proposition that grew to 28% by the start of 2024, and further to approximately 33% by early 2025.[55] In 2023 alone, the Magnificent Seven accounted for an estimated 62% of the S&P 500's 26% total return.[56] Over the decade leading up to 2024, the collective market capitalization of these seven companies grew by nearly 800%.[57]

While their market dominance is largely supported by impressive earnings growth and strong business fundamentals, the sheer scale of their influence raises valid concerns about concentration risk, market breadth, and the sustainability of such outperformance. The fundamental strength of the "Magnificent Seven" is notable. These companies generally boast significant profits, strong cash flows, and robust returns on equity, unlike many of the more speculative companies of the dot-com era or even some of the capital-intensive giants of earlier periods. This difference in fundamental underpinnings might alter the outcome or timeline of any potential mean reversion in leadership.

The narrative power associated with these "eras" of market leadership can itself contribute to concentration. As a particular group of stocks becomes widely identified as "winners", investor capital, both active and, through market-cap weighting, passive—tends to flow toward them. This can reinforce their outperformance and valuation expansion, at least for a period, creating a self-fulfilling dynamic that historically has not proven infinite.

Crucially, the shift in market leadership between these distinct eras of concentration—from the industrial and consumer giants of the Nifty Fifty era to the TMT-focused leaders of the dot-com boom, and now to the AI and platform-centric Magnificent Seven—underscores the dynamic nature of the "vital few". The Pareto Principle may consistently manifest in terms of a few firms dominating the market landscape, but which specific firms constitute that elite group changes dramatically over time, driven by broader economic shifts, technological innovation, and Schumpeterian creative destruction. For instance, only one company from the S&P 500's top 10 in 2000, Microsoft, remained in the top 10 by the early 2020s. This constant churn at the top, despite persistent overall concentration, implies that while the effect (a Pareto-like distribution of market value) is enduring, the causes (the specific companies embodying that concentration) are subject to the relentless forces of market evolution.

The Pareto Principle's manifestation in the S&P 500 is not solely about a few individual stocks achieving dominance, but often about a few sectors—and the leading companies within them—driving market trends and concentration. The concentration observed at the stock level is frequently a symptom of a more fundamental concentration at the sector level. When a particular sector, driven by innovation, economic shifts, or investor sentiment, vastly outperforms others, its constituent companies naturally gain market capitalization and, consequently, a larger weight in the cap-weighted S&P 500. This dynamic concentrates the index around these successful sectors and their champion companies.

The long-term cycles of sector leadership and relative decline—such as the prominence of Industrials in the mid-20th century, the rise and subsequent relative fall of Energy's weight, and the current ascent of Technology—suggest that the "vital few" stocks responsible for Pareto-like outcomes are themselves subject to broader economic and technological megatrends. No single sector has remained dominant indefinitely throughout the S&P 500's history. This implies that while the phenomenon of a few key drivers may persist, investors should anticipate shifts in which sectors are likely to produce these outsized winners over different market regimes.

The spirit of the Pareto Principle—the observation that a disproportionate share of outcomes is driven by a relatively small percentage of inputs—is indeed a persistent feature of the U.S. equity market, and specifically of the S&P 500 index. This conclusion is supported by academic research like Bessembinder's finding on long-term wealth creation by a select few stocks. The very nature of market-capitalization weightings in the S&P 500 tends to amplify this effect, as successful companies grow larger and their influence on the index naturally increases.

Statistical Equivalence of the S&P 500 and the Total U.S. Stock Market

Statistical equivalence is a method used to determine if two things are similar enough to be considered practically the same. While traditional statistics usually look for a difference (variance or deviation), equivalence testing flips the script to prove a lack of meaningful difference. In finance, the S&P 500 and the total U.S. stock market are considered statistically equivalent for most long-term investors.

While they are technically different—one has 500 stocks and the other has nearly 4,000—they behave so similarly that the difference is often "statistically insignificant" in practice. Here is why:

High Market Concentration Overlap

The S&P 500 consists of 500 of the largest companies in the US. Because both indices are market-cap weighted, the largest companies have the most influence. The S&P 500 accounts for approximately 85-90% of the total value of the US Stock Market. The remaining 3,000+ companies rarely have enough weight to pull the Total Market Index away from the S&P 500

Statistical Correlation

If you look at the daily or monthly returns of the S&P 500 vs. a Total Market Fund, the correlation coefficient is typically 0.99%. A correlation of 1.0 meaning they move exactly the same. At 0.99%, they are practically identical, if the S&P 500 goes up 1% then the Total Market typically goes up 0.99% or 1.01%. Because the difference in long-term annualized returns between the S&P 500 and the US Total Stock Market is so low, a few tenths of a percent, most advisors treat them as interchangeable for the purpose of asset allocation.

The equivalence falls apart slightly during different periods of market cycles. For example, if small companies explode in value (a small-cap rally) while tech giants flatline, the total market will outperform the S&P 500. However, in a severe crash, a total market index might see slightly deeper drawdowns than the S&P 500, as smaller companies can be more volatile.

In the language of statistics, the tracking error between the S&P 500 and the total U.S. stock market is so low that for a retail investor, the choice between them is a matter of preference rather than a fundamental change in risk or return. As a result, the S&P 500 is widely used as a proxy for the U.S. stock market.

Finally, it is worth considering a "meta-Pareto" perspective. The S&P 500 Index itself, by comprising approximately 500 of the largest and most liquid U.S. publicly traded companies, already represents a selection of the "vital few" from the thousands of companies in the total U.S. stock market, capturing over 80% of the value of all publicly traded U.S. stocks.[58] Bessembinder's research, which examines the universe of all listed stocks, reveals an extreme concentration of long-term wealth creation at this broadest level. The S&P 500, through its selection criteria, inherently captures many of these long-term winners. The further concentration observed within the S&P 500 is, therefore, a second-order Pareto effect, highlighting just how focused market leadership and value creation tend to be at multiple levels of analysis. This underscores the challenging, yet potentially rewarding, nature of equity investing, where identifying and participating in the success of a relatively small number of exceptional companies is key to long-term success as an investor.

CHAPTER 9

S&P 500 PASSIVE INVESTMENT PERFORMANCE VERSUS ACTIVE MANAGEMENT

The debate between active and passive investment management strategies has been a central theme in finance for decades. A critical tool for navigating this debate is the S&P Indices Versus Active (SPIVA) Scorecard, published semi-annually by SPDJI. Launched over 20 years ago, SPIVA's primary purpose is to provide an objective, data-driven comparison of the performance of actively managed mutual funds against their appropriate style benchmarks across various global markets and asset classes. Its longevity and consistent methodology have made it a go-to resource for investors and financial professionals evaluating the effectiveness of active management.

What distinguishes the SPIVA analysis and lends it significant credibility are its rigorous methodological adjustments designed to address common pitfalls in performance reporting. A significant issue in evaluating long-term fund performance is survivorship bias. Funds often merge or liquidate, frequently due to poor performance. Traditional databases that only include currently operating funds can present an overly optimistic picture of average active management success because the track records of failed funds are excluded. SPIVA explicitly corrects for this by including the performance of these "dead" funds in its analysis up to their point of disappearance. The scale of this issue is substantial. SPIVA research indicates that over a 20-year period, nearly 64% of U.S. domestic equity funds were either merged or liquidated. Over shorter periods, like five years, fund disappearance rates can still be around 25% for domestic equity funds.[59] By accounting for these non-survivors, SPIVA provides a more realistic assessment of the typical investor's experience with active funds.

The CRSP Survivor-Bias-Free US Mutual Fund Database is another key resource designed for this purpose, containing data on both active and delisted funds. It confirms that only ⅓ of active large-cap blended mutual funds still exist after 20 years in 2025, consistent with SPIVA data.[60]

Nassim Taleb coined the Lindy Rule or Lindy Effect. The idea is that the future life expectancy of some non-perishable things is proportional to their current age. The core idea is that the longer something has survived, the more resilient it has proven to be. It has withstood the test of time, fads, competition, and other stressors. Therefore, its longevity, the fact that it has survived, is a strong indicator of its robustness and likelihood to continue existing into the future. So if you're considering an active mutual fund, there's a good chance it won't be around in 20 years….you need to ask yourself, how long are you planning to hold it?

Active managers may deviate from their stated investment style (e.g., a large-cap growth manager investing in value or small-cap stocks). This "style drift" can make comparisons against a single benchmark misleading. SPIVA monitors funds for style consistency based on their actual holdings and compares their performance against benchmarks that more accurately reflect their investment style during the period analyzed. This ensures a more precise "apples-to-apples" comparison of manager performance relative to the appropriate market segment they were actually investing in.

The SPIVA US Scorecard provides compelling evidence regarding the performance of actively managed U.S. large-cap equity funds relative to their most common benchmark, the S&P 500 index. The findings over various time horizons reveal a clear and persistent trend:

<u>Short-Term (1 year):</u>
In the year-end 2024 SPIVA report, 65% of all active large-cap U.S. equity funds underperformed the S&P 500. This rate was slightly higher than the 60% observed in 2023 and marginally above the 64% average annual underperformance rate documented over the 24-year history of the SPIVA Scorecards.[61] While some years show slightly better results for active managers (e.g., 2022 saw a lower underperformance rate, though still a majority lagged), the single-year snapshot consistently shows a majority failing to beat the benchmark.

<u>Medium-Term (3–5 Years):</u>

As the time horizon extends, the challenge for active managers intensifies. SPIVA data consistently shows underperformance rates climbing as the length of time increases. For instance, data through mid-2023 indicated roughly 80% underperformance over 3 years and approaching 87% over 5 years for U.S. large-cap funds.[62] While specific percentages vary slightly with each report, the trend of increasing failure rates is robust.

<u>Long-Term (10–20 years):</u>

The difficulty of sustained outperformance becomes starkly evident over longer periods. Over the 10-year period ending December 2024, SPIVA data indicates a very high percentage of underperformance.[63] Complementary research from Morningstar reinforces this, finding that only 7% of active large-cap blend funds survived and outperformed their average passive counterparts over the decade ending December 2024.[64] Over the 15-year period ending December 2024, a definitive 89.5% of all active large-cap U.S. equity funds underperformed the S&P 500. A crucial finding from SPIVA reports is that across all domestic and international equity categories examined, there were no categories in which a majority of active managers outperformed their benchmarks over 15 years.

Extending this horizon further, over the 20-year period ending December 2024, an overwhelming 91.99% of active large-cap U.S. equity funds failed to beat the S&P 500. Data from mid-2023 SPIVA reports showed similar figures, with 94% of large-cap funds underperforming the S&P 500 over the prior 20 years.

Selected S&P 500 Data

ANNUAL RETURNS (2000–2025)					
Year Ending	Price Close	Price Change	Change	Total Return Change	Dividend Component
12/31/25 std annualized	**6845.50**	**963.88**	**16.39%**	**17.88%**	**1.49%**
12/31/25	6845.5	963.88	16.39%	17.88%	1.49%
12/31/24	5881.63	1111.80	23.31%	25.02%	1.71%
12/29/23	4769.83	930.33	24.23%	26.29%	2.06%
12/30/22	3839.50	-926.69	-19.44%	-18.11%	1.33%
12/31/21	4766.18	1010.11	26.89%	28.71%	1.81%
12/31/20	3756.07	525.29	16.26%	18.40%	2.14%
12/31/19	3230.78	723.93	28.88%	31.49%	2.61%
12/31/18	2506.85	-166.76	-6.24%	-4.38%	1.85%
12/29/17	2673.61	434.78	19.42%	21.83%	2.41%
12/30/16	2238.83	194.89	9.54%	11.96%	2.42%
12/31/15	2043.94	-14.97	-0.73%	1.38%	2.11%
12/31/14	2058.90	210.55	11.39%	13.69%	2.30%
12/31/13	1848.36	422.17	29.60%	32.39%	2.79%
12/31/12	1426.19	168.58	13.41%	16.00%	2.60%
12/30/11	1257.60	-0.03	-0.0025%	2.11%	2.11%
12/31/10	1257.64	142.53	12.78%	15.06%	2.28%
12/31/09	1115.10	211.85	23.45%	26.46%	3.01%
12/31/08	903.25	-565.10	-38.49%	-37.00%	1.49%
12/31/07	1468.36	50.05	3.53%	5.49%	1.96%
12/29/06	1418.30	170.01	13.62%	15.79%	2.18%
12/31/05	1248.29	36.37	3.00%	4.91%	1.91%
12/31/04	1211.92	100.00	8.99%	10.88%	1.89%
12/31/03	1111.92	232.10	26.38%	28.68%	2.30%
12/31/02	879.82	-268.26	-23.37%	-22.10%	1.27%
12/31/01	1148.08	-172.20	-13.04%	-11.89%	1.16%
12/29/00	1320.28	-148.97	-10.14%	-9.10%	1.03%

65

Table 9-1

The Time Horizon Effect

A consistent and critical theme emerging from decades of SPIVA data is that underperformance rates for active managers systematically rise as the measurement period lengthens. This observation points towards fundamental challenges inherent in active management. This increasing failure rate over time is not merely a reflection of more opportunities to fall behind. It underscores the powerful, compounding effect of costs and the difficulty of maintaining a persistent edge in information or skill. Active funds incur higher annual expenses compared to passive index funds. These fees erode returns year after year. Over extended periods, the cumulative impact of these seemingly small annual costs becomes a formidable hurdle. Concurrently, the ability of any single manager or firm to consistently identify mispriced securities or time market movements better than the collective market becomes increasingly difficult as information disseminates rapidly and competitors adapt. Thus, the probability of an active fund lagging its benchmark tends to grow over time.

The data suggests that active management's struggles are not confined to specific market environments. SPIVA results consistently show widespread underperformance regardless of whether markets are bullish or bearish, or experiencing high or low volatility. While active managers often claim an advantage during market downturns or periods of increased dispersion (a measure of the spread between the best and worst performing stocks, theoretically offering more opportunity for stock pickers), the long-term aggregate data does not support this assertion for the majority of funds. Years like 2022, despite market declines, did not fundamentally alter the long-term picture.

Investment Management Costs

The persistent underperformance of the average active mutual fund relative to passive benchmarks like the S&P 500 is a direct result of the costs associated with investment management. Understanding these costs is crucial for evaluating investment strategies.

The primary costs associated with mutual funds and exchange-traded funds (ETFs) is reflected in the expense ratio (ER). This represents the fund's annual operating costs—including management fees, administrative expenses, marketing, and other operational overhead—expressed as a percentage of the fund's average net assets. This fee is deducted directly from the fund's assets, thereby reducing the net return realized by investors. Some funds report both a "gross" ER (total costs) and a "net" ER, which reflects temporary fee waivers or reimbursements offered by the manager. A significant disparity exists between the typical expense ratios of actively managed funds and passive index funds:

Actively managed equity funds employ managers or teams who actively research, select, and trade securities with the goal of outperforming a benchmark. This intensive process incurs higher costs. Typical ERs range from approximately 0.50% to 1.50% or even higher for specialized strategies. Recent asset-weighted average ERs for active equity funds were around 0.7% to 0.6% but these figures were considerably higher in the past, averaging 1%+ in 1996.[66]

Passive Index Funds/ETFs (e.g., S&P 500 Trackers) aim simply to replicate the holding and performance of a specific index. This passive approach requires minimal research and trading, resulting in substantially lower operating costs. Typical

ERs for broad market index funds range from a low of 0% to around 0.1%.[67]

The gap is substantial, with active fund expense ratios often being more than 10x higher than their passive counterparts. Beyond the expense ratio, investors in active funds might also encounter sales charges (loads) or 12b-1 distribution fees (annual fees charged by some mutual funds to cover costs), although the trend has been towards no-load funds. Furthermore, the higher portfolio turnover typical of active management leads to greater implicit trading costs (bid-ask spreads, market impact) and potential tax inefficiencies.

CHAPTER 10

THE S&P 500'S ROLE IN AN INVESTMENT PORTFOLIO: CASE STUDY

Investment is most intelligent when it is most businesslike.

—The Intelligent Investor, Benjamin Graham

The Nevada Public Employees' Retirement System

The Nevada Public Employees' Retirement System (NVPERS)—a $64.5 billion defined benefit pension plan—demonstrates that a disciplined, low-cost investment strategy centered on broad market indices is not a simplistic default but a highly sophisticated and effective approach for large institutional fiduciaries.

The fund's foundational commitment to a U.S. equity

portfolio is composed entirely of an S&P 500 Index fund, a decision grounded in the principles of market efficiency and strategic risk management. This is complemented by an equally disciplined fixed-income allocation invested exclusively in U.S. Treasury securities, a structure designed to maximize diversification and provide a powerful hedge during periods of market stress. The fund's strategic underweight to illiquid, high-cost private market assets is a direct and logical consequence of its core philosophy emphasizing transparency, liquidity, and cost control.

NVPERS has consistently delivered investment returns that meet or exceed its long-term actuarial assumptions. More significantly, it is a high performer in its peer group. For the multi-year periods ending June 30, 2024, the fund's returns ranked in the top 3rd percentile or better among large public pension plans. This sustained performance is a direct result of NVPERS's ability to capture market returns while minimizing the corrosive drag of fees and transaction costs that plague its more complex peers.

The NVPERS model demonstrates that true investment sophistication is not measured by the number of asset classes in a portfolio or the complexity of its structure. Rather, it is demonstrated by the clarity of an institution's investment philosophy, the rigorous discipline of its execution, and consistently delivering superior net, risk-adjusted returns. NVPERS offers a compelling, evidence-based blueprint for investors.

NVPERS anchors its strategy in a handful of highly liquid, low-cost, publicly traded asset classes. Its domestic equity exposure is captured entirely through an S&P 500 Index fund, its international equity through a developed-market index, and its bond portfolio exclusively through U.S. Treasury securities. This approach is not the result of inertia or a lack of access, but a deliberate, long-standing philosophical choice.

NVPERS's investment model, far from being unsophisticated, represents a deliberate and intellectually rigorous application of core financial principles. The fund's unwavering commitment to a simple, low-cost, index-centric strategy is the very source of its success and the hallmark of its sophistication. True sophistication in institutional investing is not measured by the number of asset classes in a portfolio or the fees paid to external managers. It is measured by the clarity of a fund's philosophy, the discipline of its execution, and, ultimately, the superiority of its net, risk-adjusted returns delivered to its members.

The fund's investment philosophy compels a focus on quantifiable objectives—achieving a target long-term return with the least possible volatility—and necessitates a structure that is transparent, controllable, and cost-effective. The mandate to act with "care, skill, prudence, and diligence"[68] naturally steers the Board away from speculative, opaque, or excessively costly strategies where the value proposition is ambiguous.

The official investment philosophy of NVPERS is remarkably clear, consistent, and articulated across its policy documents. It is a philosophy of conviction, grounded in a set of time-tested principles that guide all strategic and tactical decisions. The central tenets of this philosophy can be summarized as follows:

<u>Systematic Market Exposure and Rebalancing:</u>
The philosophy's starting point is "Maintain consistent exposure to capital markets and systematically buy assets low and sell

them high."[69] This is not a statement about market timing but about disciplined rebalancing. The fund commits to maintaining its strategic asset allocation, which forces it to sell asset classes that have performed well (and are thus "high") and buy those that have performed poorly (and are thus "low") to return to its target weight.

Primacy of Asset Allocation:

NVPERS operates under the core belief that "asset allocation is the most significant factor influencing the risk and return of the investment program",[70] explaining over 90% of its historical performance. This conviction leads the fund to focus its intellectual and governance resources on establishing and maintaining the correct high-level mix of assets, rather than on the far less impactful pursuit of security selection within those asset classes.

Emphasis on Simplicity and Low Costs:

A recurring theme is the commitment to a "simple, low-cost structure" and an "uncomplicated" investment program. This is a strategic choice designed to enhance control, improve transparency, and minimize the drag of fees on long-term returns. The philosophy explicitly calls to "keep costs low" and "keep manager and asset turnover low".[71]

Index Management:

As a direct implementation of its philosophy, NVPERS emphasizes index management as the most efficient and cost-effective means of capturing market returns. The public market portions of its portfolio—U.S. stocks, international stocks, and U.S. bonds—are managed through a 100% indexed structure.

The physical manifestation of this philosophy is an asset allocation that is starkly different from that of its peers. The target allocation, as of fiscal year 2024, reflects a strong conviction in the return-generating power of public equities and the diversifying power of high-quality government bonds.

The asset allocation of NVPERS is not an arbitrary mix but a direct and logical consequence of its foundational philosophy. The Board's stated commitment to a "simple, low- cost structure" and an "uncomplicated" program is fundamentally incompatible with a heavy allocation to private market assets. Private equity, private credit, and hedge funds are, by their very nature, complex, opaque, illiquid, and carry fee structures that are orders of magnitude higher than those of public market index funds. The observed asset allocation, with its dominant weighting toward transparent, liquid, and low-cost indexed public markets, demonstrates a rare and sophisticated level of strategic consistency, where philosophy drives allocation.

At the heart of the NVPERS portfolio is an unambiguous and unwavering commitment to the U.S. equity market, executed through a single, clear mandate: "U.S. Stocks shall be invested in 100% S&P 500 Index."[72] This strategic choice is notable for its purity. It makes a singular, focused, and cost-effective allocation to the 500 leading large-cap companies that constitute the S&P 500, an index representing approximately 80% of the total U.S. stock market capitalization.

This decision is an active and sophisticated endorsement of one of the central tenets of modern finance: the Efficient Market Hypothesis (EMH). In its semi-strong form, the EMH posits that all publicly available information is already reflected in a security's price. For a market as heavily scrutinized and deeply analyzed as the U.S. large-cap equity market, this suggests that consistently identifying mispriced securities is an exceedingly difficult, if not impossible, task for active managers, especially after accounting for their higher fees and transaction costs.

The strategy reflects the fund's own foundational belief that "more than 90% of the System's investment performance since inception is explained by asset allocation".[73] This is a critical point. If the overwhelming driver of long-term outcomes is the strategic decision of how much to allocate to stocks, bonds, and other asset classes, then it follows that the Board's time, attention, and governance resources are best spent on perfecting that high-level decision. Devoting significant resources to the selection and oversight of active equity managers, whose collective impact on total fund returns is marginal at best and often negative after fees, would be an inefficient use of fiduciary capital and attention. The 100% S&P 500 Index strategy allows the Board and its small investment staff to focus on what truly matters: strategic policy and disciplined rebalancing.

The choice of the S&P 500 is more than a cost-saving tactic; it is a sophisticated form of risk management. In the world of institutional investing, portfolio risk can be deconstructed into two primary components: market risk, for which investors expect to be compensated over the long term, and idiosyncratic risks specific to a particular strategy or manager. By hiring active managers, a pension fund introduces a significant and uncompensated layer of idiosyncratic risk known as "manager risk". This includes the risk of a manager underperforming their benchmark, the risk of their investment style falling out of favor, the risk of personnel changes at the management firm, and even operational or reputational risks. These are the same risks that retail investors face when they purchase an actively managed mutual fund.

NVPERS's philosophy explicitly emphasizes an "uncomplicated structure to control the ability to meet long-term objectives".[74] The 100% S&P 500 Index strategy is a direct implementation of this principle. It systematically eliminates manager risk from the domestic equity portfolio. The fund's U.S. equity returns will, by definition, precisely track the S&P 500, minus a minimal fee. There is no uncertainty about manager performance, no need to conduct costly due diligence on dozens of potential managers, and no risk of a "star" manager's departure crippling a portion of the portfolio. This approach dramatically simplifies governance and oversight, allowing the Board and staff to focus on the macro-level decisions that drive the vast majority of returns. This is a deliberate and sophisticated trade-off, prioritizing structural integrity, cost control, and predictability over the speculative and often fruitless pursuit of manager-generated out performance.

The same intellectual rigor and commitment to simplicity that define the NVPERS equity strategy are evident in its fixed-income portfolio. The fund's policy is just as stark and unambiguous: "U.S. bonds shall be invested in 100% Barclays U.S. Treasury Index" (now the Bloomberg U.S. Treasury Index).[75] This decision, implemented in fiscal year 2015, was a deliberate strategic shift to "remove credit risk from the fixed-income allocation and increase total fund diversification". While most pension funds build fixed-income portfolios that include a mix of government bonds, corporate bonds, mortgage-backed securities, and high-yield debt to enhance yield, NVPERS has chosen a path of purity.

This Treasury-only strategy is a masterclass in understanding the true role of fixed income within a growth-oriented portfolio. By eschewing corporate bonds and other "spread" products that contain credit risk, NVPERS ensures that its bond portfolio functions as a pure "risk-off" haven. The primary purpose of this allocation is not to maximize income, but to provide a powerful counterbalance to the equity portfolio, especially during periods of market stress. In a financial crisis or severe market downturn, the weaknesses of a diversified credit portfolio are exposed. U.S. Treasury securities, conversely, are considered the ultimate "safe-haven" asset. During a crisis, investors globally engage in a "flight to safety", selling riskier assets and buying Treasuries. This influx of capital causes Treasury prices to rise as equity prices are plummeting.

True diversification is defined not by the number of different asset classes one holds, but by their negative correlation under stress. NVPERS strategically sacrifices the incremental yield offered by credit risk during stable periods in exchange for maximizing the portfolio's defensiveness and hedging effectiveness during volatile periods. This is a long-term strategic trade-off that prioritizes portfolio stability and the ability to rebalance from a position of strength over short-term yield enhancement.

Complementing the core holdings of U.S. stocks and Treasuries are smaller, satellite allocations designed to provide additional diversification. The international stock portfolio is managed with the same indexing discipline as its domestic counterpart, with a 100% allocation to the MSCI World Ex USA Index, which provides exposure to developed markets outside the U.S. The 12% allocation to private markets, composed of private equity and private real estate, represents the only actively managed and illiquid portion of the NVPERS portfolio.

Investment Returns and Conclusion

An investment philosophy, no matter how intellectually coherent, must ultimately be judged by its results. The fund has consistently delivered strong performance in both absolute and relative terms, demonstrating the power of its simple, low-cost approach across various market cycles.

For the fiscal year ending June 30, 2024, the NVPERS portfolio generated a formidable 11.94% return, net of all fees. This performance added approximately $6.9 billion in investment income and increased the fund's total assets by $6.1 billion (net of benefit payments) to $64.1 billion. More importantly, the fund's long-term returns have consistently exceeded its actuarial assumed rate of return, which currently stands at 7.25%. As of June 30, 2024, the fund's annualized net returns stood at 9.6% over five years, 8.3% over ten years, and 7.79% over twenty years.[76]

The investment program of the Nevada Public Employees' Retirement System stands as a powerful testament to the effectiveness of a strategy grounded in simplicity, discipline, and an unwavering focus on cost control. This analysis has demonstrated that the success of NVPERS is not accidental. It is the direct and predictable outcome of a coherent and deeply held philosophy executed with remarkable consistency over many years. By choosing to anchor its portfolio in low-cost, liquid index funds like the S&P 500 and pure U.S. Treasuries, NVPERS has systematically eliminated uncompensated risks, minimized the drag of fees, and simplified its governance structure. The result is a track record of investment returns that not only meets the NVPERS's long-term needs, but also places it in the absolute top tier of its far more complex and costly fund peers.

CHAPTER 11

THE CORPORATE LIFE CYCLE AND S&P 500 CONSTITUENTS

The S&P 500 is made up of American businesses. According to Professor Aswath Damodaran, businesses, much like human beings, age. This aging process, however, is not a function of "chronological age". A company's "age" is not measured from its founding date but by its operational and financial characteristics. A long-established firm can be operationally "young" if it successfully reinvents itself, while a new technology firm can mature and decline with startling speed.[77]

Professor Damodaran has created a corporate life cycle framework that serves as a "universal key" for demystifying corporate finance, valuation, and strategy. The true markers of a company's age are its operating metrics: specifically, its revenue growth, operating margins, and reinvestment policy. His model maps the evolution of revenues and earnings over time, identifying six distinct stages, each with unique challenges and financial characteristics. These phases represent a company's journey from an idea to a potential corporate giant, and its eventual decline.

The six stages are:

- Start-Up
- Young Growth
- High Growth
- Mature Growth
- Mature Stable
- Decline.

This progression is marked by key inflection points. The "lightbulb (idea) moment" ignites the Start-Up phase (1). The "product test" and "scaling-up test" define the high-stakes journey through Young Growth (2). The "Bar Mitzvah" marks the transition to High Growth (3), where the firm becomes a viable, profitable entity. The "mid-life crisis" signals the onset of maturity, where growth slows and strategic choices become paramount (4–5). Finally, "the end game" characterizes the period of Decline (6).

Each stage in the life cycle has a distinct "financial picture" that dictates its risk profile, financing needs, and valuation.

Stage 1: Start-Up

At this "idea" stage, revenues are "non-existent or negative". Operating margins are deeply negative as the firm is in a state of "cash burn". The company is all-consumed by research, development, and product testing. Financing is 100% equity, typically from "owner savings" or venture capital. The primary risk is existential: "failure risk" or the risk that the idea itself is not viable.

Stage 2: Young Growth

The company has passed its "product test" and now faces the "scaling-up test". Revenues begin to grow, but the firm often still reports significant operating losses. The firm is characterized by massive reinvestment, which is "large relative to their earnings". Cash flow remains negative as "cash needs multiply". Financing is still predominantly equity, perhaps from a recent IPO (initial public offering of stock) or new private equity rounds. The risk profile shifts from "idea risk" to "execution risk" —can the company scale its operations efficiently?

Stage 3: High Growth

This is often the "sweet spot". Revenue growth is explosive. Crucially, operating margins turn positive and are "changing (usually rising)". Earnings growth will often outpace revenue growth as the firm achieves operating leverage. Reinvestment remains high but is increasingly funded by internal cash flow. The firm is now likely public, and its debt capacity expands; the "benefits of borrowing significantly exceed costs". Cash flow hovers around neutral or slightly positive.

Stage 4: Mature Growth

Revenue growth begins to slow as the company saturates its market. Operating margins are high and stable. This stage is defined by a critical shift in cash flow. The firm generates "higher and more positive cash flows" primarily because "reinvestment needs decrease". The firm now faces "scarce" internal projects that can meet its hurdle rate and may turn to M&A to sustain growth. The financing mix is optimized to lower the cost of capital. Most importantly, "internal cash flows exceed investment needs", and the firm begins to return significant cash to owners via dividends and buybacks.

Stage 5: Mature Stable

Revenue growth flattens, stabilizing at a rate close to the overall economy's growth. Margins are high but face increasing pressure from new, disruptive competitors. The firm is a "cash cow". Reinvestment drops to "maintenance" levels, just enough to sustain existing assets. Debt is a large, stable part of the capital structure. The primary corporate finance decision is no longer about investment but "how much cash to return to owners?". The key challenge is a "mindset shift" from "playing offense" to "playing defense".

Stage 6: Decline

Revenues and operating margins are in a structural decline. Reinvestment becomes negative as the firm engages in "divesting" or selling off assets. Cash flows are augmented by this "partial liquidation". The firm actively pays down its debt. Damodaran argues forcefully against advice to "reinvent" the firm at this stage, as this often destroys capital. The optimal strategy is often to "accept decline, shrink, and even shut down", returning the remaining capital to investors who can redeploy it to firms in Stages 1–3.

The S&P 500's Inclusion Criteria Filter

The S&P 500 is widely regarded as the best single gauge of large-cap U.S. equities. However, it only represents 500 companies in the market. It is an actively curated portfolio, not a passive, neutral mirror of the economy. The S&P 500's inclusion criteria function as a powerful filter that structurally tilts the index toward the high-growth end of the Damodaran life cycle.

To be considered for inclusion, a company must meet a set of stringent financial viability criteria. Most importantly, it must have positive earnings in its most recent quarter, and the sum of its trailing four quarters' earnings must also be positive. The profitability screen is a life cycle filter. It systematically excludes Damodaran's Stage 1 (Start-Up) and Stage 2 (Young Growth). These stages are, by their very definition, characterized by negative earnings and operating losses as they invest heavily in scaling. The S&P 500 is, by construction, a "survivors" index. It is a portfolio composed only of companies that have already passed their "scaling-up test". An investor in an S&P 500 Index fund is investing in established, profitable, large-scale enterprises that have already proven their business models. Stage 4 and 5 companies focus on returning cash to shareholders. The vast majority of corporate earnings of the constituent companies of the S&P 500 are returned to shareholders in the form of share buybacks or dividends.

The phenomenon of "creative destruction" is accelerating, leading to higher "churn" in the index's constituents. Companies are passing the "profitability filter" to get on the index, but "disruption" is pushing them into "Decline" (and off the index) faster than ever before. The life cycle framework provides a powerful way to think about a business.

CHAPTER 12

THE MODERN ROLE OF SHARE REPURCHASES AND THE S&P 500

Share repurchases, or buybacks, have evolved from a niche corporate action into a primary method of capital return for publicly traded companies. Understanding their strategic and financial implications first requires a firm grasp of their execution and accounting treatment. Under U.S. Generally Accepted Accounting Principles (GAAP), the process of recording a share repurchase is not merely a clerical task; it reflects management's strategic intent for the reacquired shares and has a direct and material impact on the structure of a company's balance sheet.

Share repurchases trigger a series of predictable, and often significant, changes to a company's key financial metrics. While these changes are frequently presented as evidence of improved performance, a sophisticated analysis reveals that many of the effects are purely mechanical artifacts of the accounting process. The most immediate and widely publicized effect of a share buyback program is on per-share metrics, most notably earnings per share (EPS).

EPS = Net Income / Weighted Average Shares Outstanding

By reducing the denominator of this equation, a share repurchase mathematically increases EPS, assuming net income remains constant. This effect is a primary driver for many repurchase programs, as management teams are often incentivized to meet or exceed EPS targets. This can, however, mask underlying weakness; a company with flat or even declining net income can still report positive EPS growth simply by buying back enough shares.

Share repurchases should not be viewed in isolation but as one of three primary destinations for a company's free cash flow, alongside dividend payments and retaining cash for reinvestment in the business. The optimal capital allocation strategy is not universal; it is contingent on the company's stage in its corporate life cycle, its investment opportunity set, and its strategic objectives.

For companies in their growth phase, with a rich set of positive-NPV investment opportunities (e.g., new product R&D, capacity expansion, strategic acquisitions, etc.) retaining cash is the superior strategy. Returning capital to shareholders when it could be deployed internally at a high rate of return would be a value-destructive decision. Retaining cash is also prudent for companies in highly cyclical industries that need a financial buffer to survive downturns, or for those building a "war chest" for a transformative acquisition.

For mature companies whose markets are saturated and whose internal investment opportunities are scarce, generating high returns becomes difficult. When a company generates more cash than it can profitably reinvest (i.e., it has no available projects where the return on invested capital (ROIC) is higher than the weighted average cost of capital (WACC)), then this cash is considered "excess cash". Holding this excess cash on the balance sheet is value-destructive, as it earns a very low return (e.g., interest on short-term securities), which drags down the company's overall ROIC. In this scenario, the value-maximizing decision is to return the excess cash to shareholders via buybacks or dividends, allowing them to reinvest it in other enterprises with better growth prospects.

This decision framework evolves over a company's life cycle. Young, high-growth firms should retain all cash. As they mature and growth slows, they begin to generate excess cash, making buybacks, and eventually dividends, an appropriate strategy.

Share Buyback Trends

Share repurchases have become a dominant feature of the modern corporate finance landscape, serving as a flexible, tax-efficient, and powerful signaling tool for management. For investors and analysts, the effects of buybacks are a double-edged sword. They mechanically inflate key metrics such as earnings per share, which can create a misleading picture of operational performance if not carefully deconstructed. Simultaneously, they offer tangible benefits to taxable investors through tax deferral and provide a valuable element of choice that is not available with dividend distributions. The market generally reacts positively to repurchase announcements, interpreting them as a sign of management's confidence and a commitment to shareholder returns.

According to the Federal Reserve's Flow of Funds (Z.1) Report, the single largest source of net demand for U.S. equities over the past quarter-century has been non-financial corporations themselves, primarily through aggressive and sustained share repurchase programs. This consistent, strategically driven corporate bid stands in stark contrast to the more volatile and evolving behavior of other market participants, such as households and institutional investors.

A key trend throughout this period has been the structural shift in corporate payout policies, with buybacks consistently surpassing dividends as the preferred method of returning capital to shareholders. This preference is rooted in the greater flexibility, favorable tax treatment, and direct EPS impact offered by repurchases.

The period since 2000 has been marked by the unambiguous rise of the stock buyback as the preeminent tool for capital return among S&P 500 corporations. What was once a secondary option has evolved into a multi-trillion-dollar financial activity that now defines corporate capital allocation strategies and significantly influences equity market dynamics.

The sheer scale of share repurchases has grown dramatically over the past quarter-century. At the end of 1999, annual buybacks for S&P 500 companies stood at approximately $140 billion.[78] From that baseline, buyback expenditures have surged, punctuated by cyclical peaks and troughs, to set successive annual records. In 2018, S&P 500 companies repurchased $806 billion of their own stock.[79] After a brief dip during the COVID-19 pandemic in 2020 to $519 billion,[80] activity rebounded to $922 billion in 2022, followed by $795 billion in 2023, and a new annual record of $942 billion in 2024.[81] The total capital deployed is staggering; between 2010 and 2019 alone, publicly traded companies spent $6.3 trillion on repurchases.[82] See Table 12-1·

The primary and most sustainable source of funding for any corporate activity, including share repurchases, is the cash generated from a company's core business operations. The significant growth in S&P 500 buybacks since 2000 would not have been possible without a corresponding expansion in corporate profitability and available cash flow.

S&P 500 Share Buybacks Since 2018

S&P DOW JONES INDICES S&P 500, $ U.S. BILLIONS (PRELIMINARY IN BOLD)				
PERIOD	MARKET VALUE $ BILLIONS	AS REPORTED EARNINGS $ BILLIONS	DIVIDENDS $ BILLIONS	BUYBACKS $ BILLIONS
12 Mo Sep,' 25 Prelim.	**$57.047**	**$1,994.76**	**$664.90**	**$1,020.27**
12 Mo Sep,' 24	$48,701	$1,637.95	$616.16	$918.40
2024	$49,805	$1,771.24	$629.62	$942.55
2023	$40,039	$1,610.73	$588.23	$795.16
2022	$32,133	$1,453.43	$564,57	$922.68
2021	$40,356	$1,675.22	$511.23	$881.72
2020	$31,659	$784.21	$483.18	$519.76
2019	$26,760	$1,158.22	$485.48	$728.74
2018	$21,027	$1,119.43	$456.31	$806.41

[83] **Table 12-1**

Corporate finance principles and empirical evidence both point to earnings as the foundational fuel for capital returns. Buybacks are most often described as a use for "excess cash" or "residual cash flow"—the funds remaining after a company has met its operational needs and funded its capital expenditures (capex). This aligns with the "free cash flow theory", which indicates that mature firms with substantial cash flows but limited high-return investment opportunities should return that capital to shareholders to prevent inefficient or value-destroying investments. The period since 2000 has been characterized by a powerful trend of rising corporate profits. Despite significant drawdowns during the dot-com bust, the GFC, and the COVID-19 pandemic, the overall trajectory of S&P 500 operating earnings has been strongly positive. In recent years, earnings growth has been particularly robust, frequently outpacing lowered analyst expectations. For example, in Q1 2024, 75% of S&P 500 companies reported positive EPS surprises, and in Q2 2024, that figure rose to 79%.[84] This consistent ability to generate profits has created a vast and growing pool of capital available for deployment.

Share repurchase activity is not evenly distributed across the S&P 500. Two sectors have consistently dominated buyback spending for the past two decades: Information Technology and Financials. Even within these dominant sectors, buyback spending is incredibly top-heavy. The top 20 repurchasing companies in the S&P 500 regularly account for approximately half of all buyback expenditures.[85] This means that the aggregate buyback data is largely a reflection of the capital allocation policies of a handful of mega-cap firms. Perennial leaders on this list include Apple, Alphabet, Meta, and Nvidia.

Earnings Per Share Since 2020

QUARTER END	S&P 500 PRICE.	AS REPORTED; EARNINGS PER SHR: (ests are bottom up)	AS REPORTED EARNINGS; P/E (ests are bottom up)	12 MONTH EARNINGS PER SHARE AS REPORTED (ests are bottom up)
ESTIMATES				
12/31/2026		$81.38	23.60	$294.00
9/30/2026		$76.24	24.54	$282.73
6/30/2026		$70.84	25.70	$270.01
3/31/2026		$65.54	26.88	$258.13
12/31/2025 (46.5%)	6845.50	$70.10	28.15	$246.47
			27.77	(P/E on Dec,'25 price)
ACTUALS				
9/30/2025	6688.46	$63.52	28.58	$234.06
6/30/2025	6204.95	$58.96	27.88	$222.53
3/31/2025	5611.85	$53.89	25.90	$216.69
12/31/2024	5881.63	$57.69	27.99	$210.17
9/30/2024	5762.48	$51.99	28.77	$200.27
6/30/2024	5460.48	$53.12	27.87	$195.93
3/31/2024	5254.35	$47.37	27.45	$191.39
12/31/2023	4769.83	$47.79	24.79	$192.43
09/30/2023	4288.05	$47.65	23.27	$184.25
6/30/2023	4450.38	$48.58	24.59	$181.01
3/31/2023	4109.31	$48.41	23.46	$175.17
12/31/2022	3839.50	$39.61	22.23	$172.75
9/30/2022	3585.62	$44.41	19.17	$187.08
6/30/2022	3785.38	$42.74	19.69	$192.26
3/31/2022	4530.41	$45.99	22.89	$197.91
12/31/2021	4766.18	$53.94	24.09	$197.87
9/30/2021	4307.54	$49.59	24.56	$175.37
6/30/2021	4297.50	$48.39	27.07	$158.76

86

Table 12-2

CLOSING THOUGHTS

You never walk in the same river twice because the water is always flowing and always changing. Similarly, you never buy the same S&P 500 Index twice because the companies and the earnings that comprise it are always changing.

My Hypothesis

The S&P 500 has three significant factors that structurally drive earnings per share (EPS) higher over time, and as a result, the value of the index will go up over time:

1. Using Damodaran's corporate life cycle, a company is added to the S&P 500 that is likely to be in the high-growth part of the life cycle with increasing revenue and earnings (Stage 3), which will contribute positive earnings per share as the business grows and matures.
2. A mature business (Stages 4–5) is focused on the efficient

use of capital, potentially returning it to shareholders in the form of share buybacks, which will maintain or increase earnings per share.

3. Eventually, the S&P 500 committee will remove a company that is no longer able to maintain earnings per share growth from the index and replace it with a new company that is likely to be larger and more efficient than the one it is replacing, potentially contributing to an immediate earnings per share increase based solely on the constituent change.

One way to think about this is if you're running with a group of people and faster, fresher people join the group, they will push the pace, causing the slower runners to drop, making the overall group faster. As the market value of the companies increases, the companies that enter are operationally more mature and efficient at generating earnings per share.

Antifragile and the S&P 500

I've recently re-read Antifragile by Nicholas Nassim Taleb, it's a great book. My take on it is that we typically think of something as fragile if it breaks when exposed to variability, risk or harm. Think of a ceramic plate being dropped on a tile floor and it breaking. Something is robust when it can experience this variability, risk or harm and survive, think of a plastic plate being dropped on a tile floor, it won't break so it's robust. The concept of anti-fragile is that something can improve or get stronger when it is exposed to variability, risk or harm.

I visualize this as a number line where fragile is on the left side represented by -1, robust is in the middle represented by 0 and antifragile is on the right, represented by +1. The more something is anti-fragile, the more positive will be the response to variability, risk or harm, the thing will actually improve with exposure to risk. On the other hand, if something is fragile, the more it is exposed to variability, risk or harm, the worse it becomes, potentially ceasing to exist.

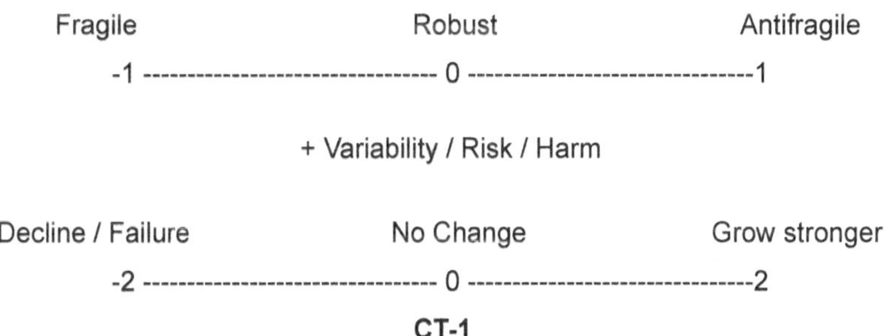

In Antifragile, Nassim Taleb uses the "Restaurant vs. City" analogy to explain how a system can be antifragile even when its individual components are fragile. When applied to the S&P 500 and its constituent companies, the logic holds that the collective index benefits from the very volatility and failures that destroy its parts.

The Analogy: Restaurants and the City

Taleb argues that the restaurant industry in a city like New York is antifragile because the individual restaurants are incredibly fragile.

<u>The Individual (Fragile):</u>
A single restaurant is sensitive to every shock, a bad review, a rent hike or a change in food trends. Most restaurants fail within a few years.

<u>The System (Antifragile):</u>
The city's culinary scene as a whole gets better because of these failures. Every time a restaurant goes bust, it leaves behind a lesson, a trained chef, or a vacant space for a better, more adapted concept to take its place. The "stress" of competition ensures that only the best survive.

Application: Companies and the S&P 500

The S&P 500 functions as the "City," and the 500 constituent companies are the "Restaurants". A company is fragile. It is vulnerable to competition, disruption, bad management, obsolescence, etc...The stress created by the competition, industry shifts, market factors, etc.. can lead to bankruptcy. The goal of the company is to not only survive but adapt and thrive, most don't. The S&P 500 is Antifragile and it benefits from the "creative destruction" of its constituents. Volatility triggers a rebalancing where weak firms are consumed by stronger firms, shrink and are moved down to the mid or small cap index, or go out of business altogether while being replaced by newer, stronger firms that are growing and leading the way in their field. This leads to a continuous improvement of the overall quality of the index.

<u>Why the S&P 500 is Antifragile</u>
The S&P 500 is not just a collection of stocks; it is an algorithmic process for harvesting the upside of capitalism while shedding the downside of individual firm failures. Just as a city is better off because "bad" restaurants fail, the S&P 500 is better off because it removes companies that are shrinking, in decline or no longer leading the way. (like Sears or GE in later years) and

replaces them with companies that are thriving (like Nvidia or Netflix). For the index, the decline of a component company is not a tragedy; it is " information" that the membership in the index should be reallocated and put to better use. The index has limited downside to any one company (a stock can only go to zero), but unlimited upside (a winner can grow 10,000+%). By constantly adding winners and removing losers, the index gains from disorder. It is the fragility of the individual companies, their ability to be removed and replaced by the Index Committee, that makes the S&P 500 antifragile.

<u>So what should you do?</u>

1. Buy a low-cost S&P 500 Index Fund or ETF. I recommend Vanguard's S&P 500 Index tracking mutual fund VFIAX or the ETF equivalent, VOO. There are many low-cost options, use the VOO expense ratio of 0.03% as a benchmark when evaluating costs for comparable S&P 500 funds.[87]

2. Determine your asset allocation between the S&P 500 and short-term Treasuries. As highlighted in the Introduction to this book, Warren Buffett recommended 90% S&P 500 and 10% short-term Treasuries for his wife, but I prefer a bit more conservative allocation at 70% S&P 500 and 30%Short Term US Treasuries.

3. Avoid debt, invest consistently, set up the investments so they are made automatically, rebalance annually—sell the fund that is above your target allocation % and use the proceeds to buy the other fund. I like to rebalance around my birthday. It takes less than 10 minutes, and I will never forget it.

4. You can withdraw 0.4% of your total investment balance each month for spending if needed. If your investment balance is $1,000,000 then you can withdraw $4,000 per month.[88]

ACKNOWLEDGEMENT

I would like to thank Howard K. Silverblatt for helping with the data compilation for this book. Howard worked for S&P for 49 years, retiring in January 2026.

"In my 49 years at S&P (May 1977–January 2026): 9.19% annualized stock return and 12.14% annualized total return; last person standing."

—Howard K. Silverblatt
Legendary S&P 500 Index Senior Analyst

ENDNOTES

[1]International Monetary Fund (IMF), estimates reported by Worldometer, 2025
[2]Office of Governor Gavin Newsom, "California Is Now the 4th Largest Economy in the World," State of California, April 23, 2025, https://www.gov.ca.gov/2025/04/23/california-is-now-the-4th-largest-economy-in-the-world
[3]S&P Global, Annual Report 2024 (New York: S&P Global, 2024), https://www.spglobal.com/en/annual-reports/2024
[4]Berkshire Hathaway Inc., "Shareholder Letters," accessed 2 February, 2026, https://www.berkshirehathaway.com/letters/letters.html
[5]S&P Global, "S&P 500 Market Attributes," accessed January 31, 2026, https://www.spglobal.com/sp-500-market-attributes-webfile
[6]S&P Global, 2024 Form 10-K Filings, GICS methodology document, October 2025.
[7]SPDJI, S&P U.S. Indices Methodology, January 2026
[8]S&P Global, "Our History," accessed February 2, 2026, https://www.spglobal.com/en/our-history

---

[9]New Market Yardstick; An Explanation of 500-Stock Index Just Begun by Wall Street Experts, New York Times, March 5, 1957, https://www.nytimes.com/1957/03/05/archives/new-market-yardstick-an-explanation-of-500stock-index-just-begun-by.html
[10]Nasdaq, "Dow Jones: Relevant Benchmark or Relic of the Past?" accessed February 2, 2026, https://www.nasdaq.com/articles/dow-jones-relevant-benchmark-or-relic-past
[11]SPDJI, Where It All Began, PDF document, accessed February 2, 2026, https://www.spglobal.com/spdji/en/documents/education/spdji-where-it-all-began.pdf

---

[12]"500-Stock Prices Digested Every Hour on the Hour: Electronic Index," New York Times, February 28, 1957, https://www.nytimes.com/1957/02/28/archives/500-stock-prices-digested-every-hour-on-the-hour-electronic-index.html

---

[13]SPDJI, "S&P 500 Index," accessed December 31, 2025, https://www.spglobal.com/spdji/en/indices/equity/sp-500/#overview
[14]S&P Global, S&P 500 Market Attributes Web File, Excel file, 2026

[15] https://www.spglobal.com/spdji/en/research/article/the-liquidity-landscape-trading-linked-to-sp-dji-indices-in-2024

[16] SlickCharts, "S&P 500 Returns Details," accessed February 2, 2026, https://www.slickcharts.com/sp500/returns/details

[17] Trade That Swing. "Average Historical Stock Market Returns for S&P 500: 5-Year Up to 150-Year Averages." Accessed February 2, 2026. https://tradethatswing.com/average-historical-stock-market-returns-for-sp-500-5-year-up-to-150-year-averages/

[18] Bankrate, "Average Stock Market Return," accessed February 2, 2026, https://www.bankrate.com/investing/average-stock-market-return

---

[19] SPDJI, Methodology: S&P U.S. Indices, PDF document, accessed February 2, 2026, https://www.spglobal.com/spdji/en/documents/methodologies/methodology-sp-us-indices.pdf

[20] Bankrate, "S&P 500 Stocks: List of Additions and Removals in 2025," accessed February 2, 2026, https://www.bankrate.com/investing/s-p-500-stocks-list-of-additions

[21] SPDJI, Index Governance Policies Methodology, PDF document, March 2025, accessed February 2, 2026, https://www.spglobal.com/spdji/en/documents/index-policies/sp-index-governance-policies.pdf

---

[22] Encyclopedia Britannica, Inc., "What Was Black Monday?" video, Britannica, accessed February 2, 2026, https://www.britannica.com/video/what-was-Black-Monday/-291786

[23] U.S. Securities and Exchange Commission, Testimony Concerning the Severe Market Disruption on May 6, 2010, testimony by Mary L. Schapiro, May 11, 2010, PDF document, accessed February 2, 2026, https://www.sec.gov/news/testimony/2010/ts051110mls.pdf

[24] Nasdaq, "Market Wide Circuit Breaker," NASDAQtrader.com, accessed February 2, 2026, https://www.nasdaqtrader.com/trader.aspx?id=CircuitBreaker

[25] U.S. Securities and Exchange Commission, Equity Market Volatility (research note, December 2015), PDF document, accessed February 2, 2026, https://www.sec.gov/marketstructure/research/equity_market_volatility.pdf

[26] Vanguard, "Vanguard Announces the Passing of Founder John C. Bogle," Vanguard Corporate Pressroom, January 16, 2019, accessed February 2, 2026, https://corporate.vanguard.com/content/corporatesite/us/en/corp/who-we-are/pressroom/Press-Release-Vanguard-Announces-Passing-Of-Founder-Jack-Bogle-011619.html

[27] YCharts, "Vanguard 500 Index Fund Admiral (VFIAX) Total Assets Under Management," accessed February 2, 2026, https://ycharts.com/mutual_funds/M%3AVFIAX/total_assets_under_management

[28] SPDJI, Float Adjustment Methodology, PDF document, April 2025, accessed February 2, 2026, https://www.spglobal.com/spdji/en/documents/methodologies/methodology-sp-us-indices.pdf

[29] David John Marotta, "Black Monday Bear: The Bear Market of 1987," Forbes,

May 21, 2018, accessed February 2, 2026, https://www.forbes.com/sites/
davidmarotta/2018/05/21/black-monday-bear-the-bear-market-of-1987/

[30]GlobalSecurity.org, "Crash of 1987," accessed February 2, 2026, https://www.
globalsecurity.org/military/world/usa/history/crash-of-1987.htm

[31]Research Affiliates, The AI Boom vs. the Dot-Com Bubble: Have We Seen This
Movie Before? PDF document, March 2025, accessed February 2, 2026, https://
www.researchaffiliates.com/content/dam/ra/publications/pdf/1038-ai-boom-dot-com-
bubble-seen-this-before.pdf

[32]Nasdaq, "Tech Giants' Market Concentration Echoes Dot-Com Bubble Peak,
Analysts Warn," Nasdaq.com, accessed February 2, 2026, https://www.nasdaq.com/
articles/tech-giants-market-concentration-echoes-dot-com-bubble-peak-analysts-
warn

[33]S&P Global, S&P Market Attributes Web File, data file, accessed February 2, 2026,
https://www.spglobal.com/spdji/en/indices/equity/sp-500/#overview

[34]Ben Carlson, "Coronavirus Stock Market Predictions: What Comes After a Bear
Market?" Fortune, March 19, 2020, accessed February 2, 2026, https://fortune.
com/2020/03/19/coronavirus-stock-market-predictions-bear-market-stocks-bottom-
what-to-expect/

[35]Investment Company Institute, The Impact of COVID-19 on Economies and
Financial Markets: Report of the COVID-19 Market Impact Working Group
(Washington, DC: Investment Company Institute, October 2020), PDF document,
accessed February 2, 2026, https://www.ici.org/files/2020/20_rpt_covid1.pdf

[36]Shiyang Huang, Bart Z. Yueshen, and Cheng Zhang, "Derivatives and Market (II)
liquidity," Journal of Financial and Quantitative Analysis 59, no. 1 (February 2024):
157–94, https://doi.org/10.1017/S0022109023000224

[37]SPDJI, Global Industry Classification Standard (GICS) Methodology, October 2025,
PDF document, accessed February 2, 2026, https://www.spglobal.com/spdji/en/
documents/methodologies/methodology-gics.pdf

---

[38]Michael Kemp, "Some Thoughts about Stock Picking," InvestmentMarkets, August
18, 2025, accessed February 2, 2026, https://www.investmentmarkets.com.au/
articles/investor-education/some-thoughts-about-stock-picking-372

[39]Visual Capitalist, "Charted: S&P 500 Market Concentration Over 145 Years,"
VisualCapitalist.com, March 3, 2025, accessed February 2, 2026, https://www.
visualcapitalist.com/charted-sp-500-market-concentration-over-145-years/

[40]Ibid

[41]S&P Global, S&P Market Attributes Web File, accessed February 2, 2026, https://
www.spglobal.com/spdji/en/indices/equity/sp-500/#overview

[42]Visual Capitalist, "Charted: S&P 500 Market Concentration Over 145 Years,"
VisualCapitalist.com, March 3, 2025, accessed February 2, 2026, https://www.
visualcapitalist.com/charted-sp-500-market-concentration-over-145-years/

[43]Ibid

44Ibid

45Sasirekha Subramanian, "The Top 10 S&P 500 Stocks By Weight—A Boon Or Bane?" Forbes, May 22, 2024, updated December 8, 2025, accessed February 2, 2026, https://www.spglobal.com/spdji/en/indices/equity/sp-500/#overview

46Visual Capitalist, "Charted: S&P 500 Market Concentration Over 145 Years," VisualCapitalist.com, March 3, 2025, accessed February 2, 2026, https://www.visualcapitalist.com/charted-sp-500-market-concentration-over-145-years/

47Sasirekha Subramanian, "The Top 10 S&P 500 Stocks By Weight—A Boon Or Bane?" Forbes, May 22, 2024, updated December 8, 2025, accessed February 2, 2026, https://www.spglobal.com/spdji/en/indices/equity/sp-500/#overview

48Dominic Pappalardo, "Morningstar Details 2 Forces That Could Derail a Stock Market That's Historically Dependent on Big Tech," Business Insider, August 2025, accessed February 2, 2026, https://finance.yahoo.com/news/morningstar-details-2-forces-could-173502756.html

49Wedbush Securities, "MarketMinute: The NVIDIA Paradox—How a Single Stock Became the S&P 500's Greatest Strength and Its Biggest Vulnerability," FinancialContent Markets, December 22, 2025, accessed February 2, 2026, https://markets.financialcontent.com/wedbush/article/marketminute-2025-12-22-the-nvidia-paradox-how-a-single-stock-became-the-s-and-p-500s-greatest-strength-and-its-biggest-vulnerability

50Sasirekha Subramanian, "S&P 500 Weight: Mag 7 Stocks and Diversification Risk," Forbes, July 7, 2025, accessed February 2, 2026, https://www.forbes.com/sites/investor-hub/article/sp-500-weight-mag-7-stocks-diversification-risk/

51Shani Jayamanne, "Investors Should Know About This Market Crash," Morningstar Australia, October 22, 2025, accessed February 2, 2026, https://www.morningstar.com.au/markets/investors-should-know-about-this-market-crash

52Gary Smith, Nifty Fifty (Pomona College Economics Files), accessed February 2, 2026, https://www.garysmithn.com/papers

53James K. Glassman, "3 Lessons for Investors From the Tech Bubble," Kiplinger, March 10, 2025, accessed February 2, 2026, https://www.kiplinger.com/article/investing/t058-c016-s002-3-lessons-for-investors-from-the-tech-bubble.html

54Shani Jayamanne, "Investors Should Know About This Market Crash," Morningstar Australia, October 22, 2025, accessed February 2, 2026, https://www.morningstar.com.au/markets/investors-should-know-about-this-market-crash

55Sasirekha Subramanian, "S&P 500 Weight: Mag 7 Stocks and Diversification Risk," Forbes, July 7, 2025, accessed February 2, 2026, https://www.fool.com/research/magnificent-seven-sp-500/

56Phil D'Iorio, "Should We Worry about the Narrow Breadth and Market Concentration in the S&P 500?" Cumberland Private (March 1, 2024), accessed February 2, 2026, https://cumberlandprivate.com/should-we-worry-about-the-narrow-breadth-and-market-concentration-in-the-sp-500/

57Lyle Daly, "The Magnificent Seven's Market Cap vs. the S&P 500," The Motley

Fool, updated January 5, 2026, accessed February 2, 2026, https://www.fool.com/research/magnificent-seven-sp-500/

---

[58]SPDJI, S&P 500® Brochure: The Gauge of the U.S. Large-Cap Market, accessed February 2, 2026, https://www.spglobal.com/spdji/en/indices/equity/sp-500/#overview

---

[59]S&P Dow Jones Indices, "SPIVA® (S&P Indices Versus Active)," accessed February 2, 2026, https://www.spglobal.com/spdji/en/research-insights/spiva/
[60]Center for Research in Security Prices (CRSP), CRSP Survivor-Bias-Free U.S. Mutual Funds Database, accessed February 2, 2026, https://www.crsp.org/research/crsp-survivor-bias-free-us-mutual-funds/
[61]S&P Dow Jones Indices, "SPIVA® (S&P Indices Versus Active)," S&P Dow Jones Indices Research & Insights, accessed February 2, 2026, https://www.spglobal.com/spdji/en/research-insights/spiva/
[62]SPDJI, "SPIVA® (S&P Indices Versus Active)," SPDJI Research & Insights, accessed February 2, 2026, https://www.spglobal.com/spdji/en/research-insights/spiva/
[63]Ibid
[64]Morningstar, U.S. Active/Passive Barometer Report: Mid-Year 2025, PDF report, accessed February 2, 2026, https://marketing.morningstar.com/content/cs-assets/v3/assets/blt9415ea4cc4157833/blt571aae8649fe75ee/680a4be24d5bf0461e2676c3/H1_2025_US_Active_Passive_Barometer_Report.pdf
65 S&P Global, S&P 500 Market Attributes Web File 2, accessed February 2, 2026
66Investment Company Institute, "Mutual Fund Expense Ratios Down Sharply from a Quarter Century Ago," news release, March 24, 2022, Investment Company Institute, accessed February 2, 2026, https://www.ici.org/news-releases/22-news-trends
[67]Bankrate, "Low-Cost Index Funds: A Beginner's Guide," Bankrate, accessed February 2, 2026, https://www.bankrate.com/investing/low-cost-index-funds-guide/

---

[68]Public Employees' Retirement System of Nevada, Official Policies, effective September 1, 2024, PDF document, accessed February 2, 2026, https://www.nvpers.org/sites/default/files/2024-10/2024-PERSOfficialPolicies-Final.pdf
[69]Ibid
[70]Ibid
[71]Ibid
[72]Ibid
[73]Ibid
[74]Ibid
[75]Ibid
[76]Ibid

---

[77]Aswath Damodaran, Corporate Life Cycle: Class Introduction, PDF lecture slides,

accessed February 2, 2026, https://pages.stern.nyu.edu/~adamodar/pdfiles/CLC/slides/CLCclassintro.pdf

[78]SPDJI, S&P 500 Buyback, Excel spreadsheet, accessed February 2, 2026, https://www.spglobal.com/spdji/en/documents/additional-material/sp-500-buyback.xlsx

[79]CFA Institute, Stock Buybacks: A Literature Review, PDF document, 2022, accessed February 2, 2026, https://www.cfainstitute.org/sites/default/files/-/media/documents/book/rf-lit-review/2022/rflr-stock-buybacks.pdf

[80]Ibid

[81]S&P Dow Jones Indices, "S&P 500 Q4 2024 Buybacks Increase 7.4% and 2024 Expenditure Sets New Record by Increasing 18.5%," S&P Dow Jones Indices News, accessed February 2, 2026, https://www.spglobal.com/spdji/en/corporate-news/article/sp-500-q4-2024-buybacks-increase-74-and-2024-expenditure-sets-new-record-by-increasing-18-5

[82]U.S. Securities and Exchange Commission, Comment Letter on Proposed Rule S7 21 21, PDF document, December 20, 2005, accessed February 2, 2026, https://www.sec.gov/comments/s7-21-21/s72121-20122005-275317.pdf

[83]S&P Global, S&P 500 Market Attributes Web File 2, accessed February 2, 2026

[84]FactSet Research Systems, Earnings Insight: May 17, 2024, PDF document, accessed February 2, 2026, https://advantage.factset.com/hubfs/Website/Resources%20Section/Research%20Desk/Earnings%20Insight/EarningsInsight_051724A.pdf

[85]S&P Dow Jones Indices, "S&P 500 Q1 2024 Buybacks Increase 8.1% from Q4 2023; 12 Month Expenditure Declines," S&P Dow Jones Indices Corporate News, June 17, 2024, accessed February 2, 2026, https://www.spglobal.com/spdji/en/corporate-news/article/sp-500-q1-2024-buybacks-increase-81-from-q4-2023/

[86]S&P Global, S&P 500 Market Attributes Web File 2, accessed February 2, 2026

---

[87]The Vanguard Group, Vanguard Institutional Index Fund Fact Sheet (F0968), PDF document, accessed February 2, 2026, https://institutional.vanguard.com/assets/corp/fund_communications/pdf_publish/us-products/fact-sheet/F0968.pdf

[88]Bill Bengen Revisits The 4% Rule Using Shiller's CAPE Ratio, Michael Kitces Research, accessed February 2, 2026, https://www.fa-mag.com/news/choosing-the-highest--safe--withdrawal-rate-at-retirement-57731.html

ADVANCED PRAISE

"An intriguing and fact-filled study of an investing cornerstone, the S&P 500 index. Written in plain English, with an abundance of useful and interesting information. A must for the aspiring investor, a treat for the experienced one."

—Bill Bengen, author of "A Richer Retirement, Supercharging the 4% Rule to Spend More and Enjoy".

"This book is a fascinating and fun read that will give you much needed background on the history and construction of the S&P 500 index, and make you a more informed investor."

—Aswath Damodaran, Professor at NYU, Stern School of Business

"It is not merely a handbook on the S&P 500. It is an argument that the index is one of the great hidden machines of modern life: part scorekeeper, part filtration system, part evolutionary mechanism, part civic myth."

—Demetris Papadimitropoulos, Reviewer